THE GIFT

THE MIRACLE OF UNEXPECTED ABUNDANCE

BENNY HINN

Bookmark
PUBLISHING

DALLAS, TEXAS

THE GIFT
© 2008 by Bookmark Publishing

Published by Bookmark Publishing
P.O. Box 610010
Dallas, TX 75261

All Scripture quotations, unless otherwise indicated, are taken from the *King James Version.*

Scripture quotations marked (NIV) are taken from the *Holy Bible, New International Version,* NIV®, Copyright © 1973, 1978, 1984 by International Bible Society. Used by permission of Zondervan Publishing House. All rights reserved.

ISBN: 1-59024-361-7

www.BennyHinn.org

Printed in the United States of America.

2008—First Edition
10 9 8 7 6 5 4 3 2 1

CONTENTS

INTRODUCTION

Let me prepare you! This is not an ordinary book concerning God's desire to bless His children. What you are about to read is the story of how the Lord performs the miraculous in order to bring unexpected abundance.

I'm eager to share what God's Word tells us about seven great wealth transfers. Six have already taken place, and one is on its way!

Why do I believe such a divine gift is imminent? Because the timing, conditions, and atmosphere are all falling into line, yet there are requirements and conditions which must be obeyed—and they are clearly stated in His Word.

Even though God mentions money, riches, and wealth over two thousand times in the Bible, His abundance includes much more than financial resources. The Lord is ready to pour out unforeseen blessings on every area of your life.

On these pages I want to share these helpful points:

- Six steps to receiving God's favor
- How to sow your way out of a crisis
- The three keys of preparation for the coming wealth transfer
- How to open the door for a miracle
- What God says concerning making vows and covenants
- How you can receive the seven gifts of blessing
- The secret of living without lack

The wealth transfer the Lord is preparing requires that you be moved by faith rather than reason, by hope instead of fear, by obedience rather than doubt.

Now I want to help you get ready for what is about to occur. God has a special gift for YOU!

— BENNY HINN

1

A Supernatural Wealth Transfer

As a usually very active six-year-old, I was now patiently waiting in the living room of our house in Jaffa, Israel, for my father to return from a business trip to Cyprus.

Dad had a rather stern demeanor—a man who didn't show his emotions easily—yet, as one of his eight children, I knew how much he loved us.

This particular day, on his arrival home, my father, Costandi, opened a bag he was carrying and presented a little toy gun he had purchased especially for me.

I can still see it in all its splendor—about twelve inches long and sparks would fly every time I pulled the trigger.

You can imagine my heartbreak when, two days

later, my brother Chris took my prized possession from me and broke it. I thought I would never stop crying.

I now realize that small inexpensive toy gun was one of my most cherished gifts, because it was from my dad.

Finances for the Tabernacle

What I am excited to share with you concerns a gift which is like none other, and it is received from your heavenly Father. It is an incredible wealth transfer such as the world has never seen. And those who receive it will be specially chosen by God. If you are a born again believer, this transfer can include you!

———— ∾ ————

If you are a born again believer,
this transfer can include you!

Let's begin by turning our attention to an event which occurred thousands of years ago.

When the children of Israel were leaving the bondage of Egypt and heading for the Promised Land, the Almighty knew they would need finances to survive the journey.

I am not referring to a natural, physical survival, but one which is spiritual. As we will see, there was to be a Tabernacle built.

Without it, the glory would not have descended, nor would God have dwelt with His people. Their survival was because of God's abiding presence.

The Lord declared to Moses, *"And let them make me a sanctuary; that I may dwell among them"* (Exodus 25:8).

Prior to this, the Lord had instructed Moses to go to a mountain by himself (Exodus 19:3). There, his meeting with the Almighty was so sacred that God instructed him to tell the people, *"Take heed to yourselves, that ye go not up into the mount, or touch the border of it: whosoever toucheth the mount shall be surely put to death"* (verse 12).

There's no mention in the Bible of Moses carrying any blood to the mountain. Yet in the Tabernacle— the place of God's habitation—we read how the blood was applied to the altar (Exodus 29:12) before the people could enter.

The reason they were not able to approach the mountain is because at this time the blood was not required of Israel. God had not requested fellowship with them, just Moses alone.

When God met Moses at the burning bush there was no blood shed, and the same was true when he met the Almighty on the mountain.

It was only later, when Israel needed to approach God in His "dwelling place," that blood was required.

Jewels of Silver and Gold

The construction of God's house required finances.

That is why, before the final plague in Egypt, God told Moses:

Speak now in the ears of the people, and let every man borrow of his neighbour, and every woman of her neighbour, jewels of silver and jewels of gold. And the LORD *gave the people favour in the sight of the Egyptians. Moreover the man Moses was very great in the land of Egypt, in the sight of Pharaoh's servants, and in the sight of the people.* (Exodus 11:2-3)

And I will give this people favour in the sight of the Egyptians: and it shall come to pass, that, when ye go, ye shall not go empty. But every woman shall borrow of her neighbour, and of her that sojourneth in her house, jewels of silver, and jewels of gold, and raiment: and ye shall put them upon your sons, and upon your daughters; and ye shall spoil the Egyptians. (Exodus 3:21-22)

God arranged this incredible wealth transfer at the right moment for the right reason, and the people began their journey toward the Promised Land carrying with them the wealth of Egypt.

Prior to the first plague, I doubt Moses and the children of Israel would have been ready to receive such a divine message. But God brought them to the place of faith and informed Moses, "Now is the time!"

A Golden Idol?

I believe the moment is drawing near in God's master plan for a similar wealth transfer of unthinkable proportions, and we must prepare to receive this gift.

What you are about to learn will enable you to be in the right place at the right time for this heavenly outpouring.

However, we must be ready to answer this question: What will I do with this divine blessing?

We must be careful not to make the same mistake as Aaron. Before the Tabernacle was constructed, he was involved in persuading the children of Israel to use the incredible wealth they had accumulated for the wrong reason. They melted the gold jewelry received from the Egyptians and formed an idol in the shape of a calf (Exodus 32:2-4).

The result was God's judgment. The Lord *"plagued the people, because they made the calf, which Aaron made"* (verse 35).

Today, the wealth transfer the Lord is about to initiate is to be reserved for the spreading of the Gospel.

———— ⌇ ————

Today, the wealth transfer the Lord is about to initiate is to be reserved for the spreading of the Gospel.

If you read the Old Covenant you will discover how the people of Israel who worshiped God rather than the golden calf were spared from wrath.

The final day of judgment is at hand, and if we are careful with what rightfully belongs to the Lord —using it for His purpose, not ours—God will spare His judgment.

Abundance Requires Truth

In one of the most quoted promises of God's favor, we read, *"Beloved, I wish above all things that thou mayest prosper and be in health, even as thy soul prospereth"* (3 John 2).

However, the key which unlocks the door to heaven's blessing—and what will unleash the transfer of wealth—is *truth!* This is why we need to read the two verses which follow: *"For I rejoiced greatly, when the brethren came and testified of the truth that is in thee, even as thou walkest in the truth. I have no greater joy than to hear that my children walk in truth"* (verses 3-4).

Since biblical prosperity is the result of divine truth, it is imperative we fill our lives with God's precious Word.

A Supernatural Act

It is our human nature to desire God's abundance, yet we lack the patience to wait. We think, I'm going to sow today and will reap tomorrow.

Wrong! What we receive comes because of *His* reasons, in *His* timing.

The harvest spoken of in God's Word is not equivalent to the paycheck you will receive at the end of the week to pay your bills. That is simply an exchange for your labor.

Even the funds you invest for future dividends have nothing to do with the harvest God speaks of. In fact, there are plenty of non-Christians whose financial knowledge produces great wealth.

The reaping I am referring to is a supernatural act of God which is based on your personal obedience and faithfulness, not the result of your intelligence or abilities.

According to the Word, the riches of the world are cursed—and will eventually be destroyed.

The Seven Great
Wealth Transfers

The Word of God tells us there have already been six great wealth transfers—and one more is about to take place.

Wealth Transfer #1: Abraham

In Genesis 12:10, when famine struck the land, Abram went down into Egypt. While there, the Egyptians saw Sarai's beauty and spoke of her to Pharaoh, who decided to take her for a wife. Pharaoh gave Abram many gifts (verse 16), including oxen, servants, cattle, and much wealth, believing Sarai was Abram's sister. However, when Pharaoh discovered she was actually his wife (after the Lord had plagued the Egyptian ruler), he eventually returned her to Abram.

The Bible tells us, *"And Abram went up out of Egypt, he, and his wife, and all that he had, and Lot with him, into the south. And Abram was very rich in cattle, in silver, and in gold"* (Genesis 13:1-2).

This was the first recorded transfer of riches from the wicked to the righteous.

Wealth Transfer #2: Isaac

Once again there was famine in the land, and Isaac went to Abimelech of the Philistines—and God granted him favor. Scripture records these amazing facts: *"Then Isaac sowed in that land, and received in the same year an hundredfold: and the LORD blessed him. And the man waxed great, and went forward, and grew until he became very great: For he had possession of flocks, and possession of herds, and great store of servants: and the Philistines envied him"* (Genesis 26:12-14).

Please note that these transfers took place in times of famine and hardship. This means your prosperity is not dependent on the world's conditions, but on the Word of God.

Wealth Transfer #3: Jacob

The Lord gave Jacob the wealth of his difficult father-in-law, Laban. Jacob said to Rachel and Leah, *"And ye know that with all my power I have served your father. And your father hath deceived me, and changed my wages ten times; but God suffered him not to hurt me. If he said thus, The speckled shall be thy wages; then all the cattle bare speckled: and if he said thus, The ringstreaked [streaked animals] shall be thy hire; then bare all the cattle ringstreaked. Thus God hath taken away the cattle of your father, and given them to me"* (Genesis 31:6-9).

Wealth Transfer #4: Joseph

Joseph received the riches of Egypt:

And Pharaoh said unto Joseph, Forasmuch as God hath showed thee all this, there is none so discreet and wise as thou art: Thou shalt be over my house, and according unto thy word shall all my people be ruled: only in the throne will I be greater than thou. And Pharaoh said unto Joseph, See, I have set thee over all the land of Egypt. And Pharaoh took off his ring from his hand, and put it upon Joseph's hand, and arrayed him in vestures of fine linen, and put a gold chain about his neck; And he made him to ride in the second chariot which he had; and they cried before him, Bow the knee: and he made him ruler over all the land of Egypt. And Pharaoh said unto Joseph, I am Pharaoh, and without thee shall no man lift up his hand or foot in all the land of Egypt. (Genesis 41:39-44)

Imagine! God bestowed upon Joseph the wealth and treasure of an entire nation. So much so that Pharaoh told Joseph he was now in control of all business and economy in the land.

Wealth Transfer #5: Israel

Egypt was an extremely prosperous nation during the time the children of Israel were slaves under Pharaoh. It was the superpower of the day!

Yet, after suffering through ten plagues and the transfer of wealth to the Israelites (which we discussed earlier in this chapter), when Moses led the great exodus, Egypt was left in a state of bankruptcy.

During the previous four-hundred-plus years, the Lord had a reason for allowing the Egyptians to succeed in business and commerce. Why? Because the money was being accumulated and reserved specifically for God's people.

Israel was the recipient of a supernatural harvest they never worked for, but prayed and *believed* for.

It is vital to remember that the transfer did not happen until Moses appeared on the scene as God's chosen leader and declared, "Thus saith the Lord."

For centuries the Word of God had not been preached among the Israelite slaves in Egypt. There was no truth being disseminated.

It was the Word spoken through Moses which eventually brought God's presence and deliverance.

The result was a reassigning of riches for the Father's purpose.

Wealth Transfer #6: King Solomon

God Almighty not only gave Solomon the treasures of one nation, but the multiplied wealth of the world. The Bible declares, *"So king Solomon exceeded all the kings of the earth for riches and for wisdom"* (1 Kings 10:23).

Wealth Transfer #7: You

Who is next in line to receive unexpected abundance? It's you!

———— ∼ ————

Who is next in line to receive unexpected abundance? It's you!

God's Word clearly states, *"The wealth of the sinner is [being] laid up for the just"* (Proverbs 13:22).

In Deuteronomy 8:18 we are told, *"But thou shalt remember the LORD thy God: for it is he that giveth thee power to get wealth, that he may establish his covenant which he sware unto thy fathers, as it is this day.*"

The reason the Lord desires to give us the wealth of the sinner is to establish His covenant—the Gospel of Jesus Christ, His Son, for the nations. God is going to bless you in this manner so you can support the preaching of the Gospel to the entire world!

The Coming Outpouring

As the daily headlines read and the news anchors blare, it is obvious we are living in dangerous times. The world is headed toward disaster—war, climate changes, hunger, famine, drought, over-population, and the poisoning of our planet. In addition, there is evil on earth caused by satanic forces.

However, before total catastrophe strikes, there will be a moment of brightness where the Gospel will be proclaimed. God will send a mighty revival to a world in crisis to rescue humanity.

Here is an amazing question posed by Jesus: "*When the Son of man cometh, shall he find faith on the earth?*" (Luke 18:8).

Jesus wasn't talking of His church, rather, He's

asking if humanity will believe there is a higher power with ultimate authority?

"Who Needs God?"

All around us there is a growing godless mentality.

With medical science claiming they will eliminate sickness from the face of the earth, many are saying, "Who needs God?"

However, let's not forget that what took place in Bible days is a prophetic picture of what is happening in our day. Those who built the Tower of Babel announced, "We don't need God. We can do anything we want."

Even when the church of Jesus Christ is raptured, millions will still refuse to believe there is a God in heaven. As disaster begins to strike they will blaspheme the Creator.

A Quick Work

As believers, we are being prepared for the moment when the Gospel will be preached everywhere with great intensity.

As a result, humanity will look to God for a season

and then deny Him. During this time, the Lord will sweep the earth with unprecedented power. Today, as I watch the ways of the Spirit, I can see the pieces of a puzzle being put together.

The Lord is allowing certain events to take place which will climax with the world's cry, "We need God now."

At that moment the Gospel will rain down as a sudden blessing from heaven. But this will not last long because the Lord has promised to pour out *"the former rain, and the latter rain"* in the same month (Joel 2:23). Yes, God will do a quick work.

This prophetic statement speaks of a rapid move of God which will sweep the land. The Almighty will use present-day technology and the tools He has allowed men to create for the spreading of the Gospel. I believe when this happens, it will occur with such suddenness that the body of Christ will respond to the voice of the Spirit and support this quick move with literally billions of dollars. A flood of finances will be released.

Prior to this time, God will bring about "The Gift" —a wealth transfer like nothing we can dare to imagine.

More Than Enough

This is no different than God saying to Moses, "Build me a Tabernacle now."

Concurrently, the Lord instructed Moses to tell the people, *"Bring me an offering. You are to receive the offering for me from each man whose heart prompts him to give"* (Exodus 25:2, NIV).

There was such an outpouring of giving for the building of the Tabernacle that Moses finally sent this word throughout the camp: *"No man or woman is to make anything else as an offering for the sanctuary." And so the people were restrained from bringing more, because what they already had was more than enough to do all the work"* (Exodus 36:6-7, NIV).

I fervently believe the Almighty is about to perform this miracle again.

In Moses' day, when God's requirements were met, the people were allowed to keep the leftovers for their personal needs.

If you are faithful, you, too, will have more than enough to carry you to the Promised Land.

2

Unexpected Abundance

True biblical abundance is not an accident waiting to happen; it is something for which we must prepare. Start by confessing, *"Thy word is truth"* (John 17:17).

I believe God's divine gift is imminent because the timing, conditions, and atmosphere are all falling in line, but you and I must be obedient to what God is saying to us through His Word.

Three Keys

In the book of Job, the Almighty gives us three vital keys regarding how to prepare for the coming wealth transfer.

Key #1: Get acquainted with God.

If there is a broken relationship between you and your heavenly Father, move quickly to see your fellowship restored. Scripture tells us, *"Acquaint now thyself with him"* (Job 22:21).

Key #2: Make sure there is peace between you and the Lord.

There must be no conflict involving heaven and your soul. That is why we are instructed to *"be at peace: thereby good shall come unto thee"* (Job 22:21).

Since peace with God only comes through Christ Jesus, make certain His blood has been applied to your heart. It opens the door for every good gift the Father desires for you to possess.

Key #3: Take your instructions directly from God.

A word from God may be delivered by a third party, but we must always go to the original source. The Bible says, *"Receive, I pray thee, the law from his mouth, and lay up his words in thine heart"* (Job 22:22).

When you read the Word continually, you establish a direct link—a communication with God which allows Him to speak personally to you.

———— ∼ ————

When you read the Word continually, you establish a direct link—a communication with God which allows Him to speak personally to you.

It's Conditional

Something marvelous takes place when you decide to activate these three keys. We are told, *"If thou return to the Almighty, thou shalt be built up, thou shalt put away iniquity far from thy tabernacles"* (Job 22:23).

The gift God is preparing for you is conditional. Notice the first word in the above Scripture: *"If."* In other words, what the Father has in store is only for those who obey His Word and pursue His principles.

By taking these actions you will be fortified and sin

will be removed from your house. Why? Because you have invited God's presence into your midst.

These promises are the result of (1) getting acquainted with God, (2) making peace with Him, and (3) having His Word written on your heart.

Now you are ready for the transfer of heavenly treasures. As recorded in the very next verses, *"Then shalt thou lay up gold as dust, and the gold of Ophir as the stones of the brooks. Yea, the Almighty shall be thy defence, and thou shalt have plenty of silver"* (Job 22:24-25).

God's abundance will begin to permeate your life. These precious gifts are not being offered from your employer or the dividends on your investments. What is about to take place is *supernatural.*

———— ∼ ————

These precious gifts are not being offered from your employer or the dividends on your investments. What is about to take place is supernatural.

As valuable as it may be, you will not receive just ordinary gold, but the absolute *best*—the quality of the gold of Ophir. That is what was used in the great Temple built by Solomon (1 Chronicles 29:3).

The Windows Will Open!

Become a diligent student of God's Word by spending time in Scripture daily. *"For then shalt thou have thy delight in the Almighty, and shalt lift up thy face unto God. Thou shalt make thy prayer unto him, and he shall hear thee, and thou shalt pay thy vows"* (Job 22:26-27).

Think of it! You'll have enough to give the Lord what you promised!

Perhaps you will respond, "Well, I'm giving now."

While that may be true, I am talking of the day when God declares, "Now the Gospel must be preached"—and He will lay the gold and silver in your hand to multiply the Great Commission.

When that begins to be manifest, the blessings of God will rest on you so abundantly, you will experience what is written in Malachi 3:10: God will *"open...the windows of heaven, and pour you out a blessing, that there shall not be room enough to receive it."*

More Than a Suggestion

Many believers barely exist from paycheck to paycheck and are buried in debt because they have not understood the principles of the Word. The first portion of the above verse tells us, *"Bring ye all the tithes into the storehouse, that there may be meat in mine house, and prove me now herewith, saith the LORD of hosts"* (Malachi 3:10). This is not a mere suggestion, but a direct command of Jehovah God—and is the basis for our abundance.

However, the church has yet to see the reality of the "windows of heaven" being opened in the manner which is about to take place.

Let me remind you that *any* individual can create money through hard work and smart decisions, but when you are faithful to the Lord, He will place wealth in your hands you did *not* work for. He does this because He *trusts* you.

True Riches?

Jesus made this prophetic statement: *"If therefore ye have not been faithful in the unrighteous mammon, who will commit to your trust the true riches?"* (Luke 16:11).

Most people interpret true riches to mean the anointing of the Spirit and God's presence. But I am firmly convinced Jesus was speaking here of the time when real wealth will not be the result of your physical labor. Rather it is an unexpected windfall of abundance only God can provide.

Move Forward in Faith

The moment you prove yourself faithful, you place yourself in line to receive The Gift, because righteousness lifts you into a position to experience the impending supernatural harvest.

We are on the brink of this divine, God-given prosperity.

———— ∼ ————

We are on the brink of this divine, God-given prosperity.

It is much closer than we realize, and the conditions on earth are moving us toward this miraculous moment.

Without question, such an event is difficult to fathom. Can you imagine what it was like when Moses told the children of Israel—still under the bondage of Pharaoh—to ask their Egyptian neighbors for *"jewels of silver, and jewels of gold, and raiment"* (Exodus 3:22)?

It's not an easy assignment to knock on a person's door and say, "Give me your gold," but not one Israelite turned to Moses and commented, "What did you say? Are you crazy? If I ask for their jewels they may take a sword and chop my head off!"

Instead of questioning, "Should I?" they obeyed.

Why? Because miracles were happening all around them, and they knew Moses was speaking on behalf of God.

When the Lord commands, "Go," any person who is truly listening for the voice of God will move forward with faith and trust.

You Will Flourish

Right now, across the world, the Lord is preparing the hearts of His people for The Gift. The Word declares, *"Evil pursueth sinners: but to the righteous good shall be repayed"* (Proverbs 13:21).

We also know, *"The house of the wicked shall be overthrown: but the tabernacle of the upright shall flourish"* (Proverbs 14:11).

In this passage, God is referring to the fact the household of the sinner will go bankrupt, but the floodgates of abundance will open wide for the believer.

Scripture does not tell us the house of the wicked will be destroyed and the inhabitants killed. No, it is speaking of a financial transfer.

27

This same principle is declared as we read, *"In the house of the righteous is much treasure: but in the revenues of the wicked is trouble"* (Proverbs 15:6).

Under the guidance of the Holy Spirit, Solomon wrote, *"By humility and the fear of the LORD are riches, and honour, and life"* (Proverbs 22:4).

Ever-Increasing Wealth

As God's people we can't brag to the world, "I'm a smart businessperson. I did it all myself." That is not humility. Instead, we need to confess, "Lord, none of this is my doing. I'm simply a vessel You have trusted with finances to fulfill Your purpose."

The Almighty is serious concerning your commitment in this matter. He declares, *"A faithful man shall abound with blessings: but he that maketh haste to be rich shall not be innocent"* (Proverbs 28:20). One version translates it *"will not go unpunished"* (NIV).

If you read the words of this verse closely you will understand that "quick money" or making a "fast buck" is cursed.

When someone approaches you with an offer to turn your investment into instant wealth, be wary. There are deceivers—even in the church—who will convince you their "deal" is too good to pass up, but be extremely cautious. They may promote a pitch such as, "If you invest $10,000, you'll receive $1,000 every month for the next two years."

Don't be tempted by greed or you will be engulfed in trouble.

Only those who are dedicated and faithful will abound in blessings—and this is a process. If you are responsible with a little, God will give you more—and when you prove you are trustworthy, He will enrich you with ever-increasing wealth.

This makes me want to shout!

3

GET READY FOR GOD'S FAVOR

God creates every individual with unique gifts and abilities.

One of those talents may be the competence and creativity to make money in business. If this is true, God will use your success for His glory—so be faithful with your gift and make sure it is nurtured and protected. The Bible tells us, *"Whoso keepeth the fig tree shall eat the fruit thereof: so he that waiteth on his master shall be honoured"* (Proverbs 27:18).

God doesn't approve or condone laziness.

You may say, "Lord, You know I'm competent when it comes to finances—plus, I'm a good person. So I *must* be one who will receive what You are about to outpour."

God laughs at your foolishness!

The righteous are diligent. That is why the Lord is telling you, "Take care of that fig tree!"

Do You Qualify?

Whether it is our God-given attributes or spiritual blessings, we must be good stewards if we expect an increase. *"Be thou diligent to know the state of thy flocks, and look well to thy herds. For riches are not for ever: and doth the crown endure to every generation?"* (Proverbs 27:23-24).

In this verse the Lord is reminding us, "If you are talented and accumulate money or other assets, carefully look after what you have. Prove yourself faithful in the things you possess today so you can qualify for what is coming tomorrow."

Riches are a temporary gain, not guaranteed forever—and you will lose them unless you nurture your gift.

Next, we read, *"The hay appeareth, and the tender grass showeth itself, and herbs of the mountains are gathered. The lambs are for thy clothing, and the goats are the price of the field. And thou shalt have goats'* milk enough for thy food, for the food of thy household, and for the maintenance for thy maidens" (Proverbs 27:25-27).

Once more, God is reminding us, "I am going to endow you with wealth you haven't worked for. But before you receive, I am watching how you handle what I have already entrusted to your care."

The Diligence Factor

Remember, we are going to receive, because *"the wealth of the sinner is [being] laid up for the just"* (Proverbs 13:22).

The Lord is examining our efforts before He trusts us with His favor.

———————— ∼ ————————

The Lord is examining our efforts before He trusts us with His favor.

To be diligent and industrious are godly virtues.

Pay close attention to these words: *"Seest thou a man diligent in his business? he shall stand before kings; he shall not stand before mean men"* (Proverbs 22:29).

33

The term "mean men" refers to "obscure men" —those who possess no power or influence.

Will we really stand before royalty?

Remember the story of Joseph? He was sold into slavery and became a prisoner. Because Joseph was steadfast in his faith, God promoted him despite his circumstances.

———— ≈ ————

Because Joseph was steadfast in his faith, God promoted him despite his circumstances.

When Joseph worked for Photiphar, he was so industrious he was elevated to the position of overseeing the household.

Then, because of the advances of Potiphar's wife, he was thrown into prison, but he was so faithful in his assignments they placed him in charge of the entire prison. Finally he was trusted and respected to such an extent, Pharaoh announced, "I'm going to make you governor of Egypt—second in command only to me."

Even a heathen king can recognize the Holy Spirit resting on a man who is trustworthy!

Divine Promotion

Let us think for a moment about the prophet Daniel.

He was a prisoner of war in an ungodly land, but was honorable in his service to a heathen king. Because of his diligence, God promoted him to be a counselor to royalty.

Another example is Nehemiah, a cupbearer for the king of Persia. As a reward for his exemplary character, he was also lifted by God for a divine purpose.

Here is what Scripture declares: *"He becometh poor that dealeth with a slack hand: but the hand of the diligent maketh rich"* (Proverbs 10:4). We also know *"the thoughts of the diligent tend only to plenteousness"* (Proverbs 21:5).

Even the concepts, ideas, or plans of such a person lead to abundance. You are to be industrious with whatever God places in your hand—large or small.

———— ∾ ————

You are to be industrious with whatever God places in your hand—large or small.

The Word reveals what the Lord is waiting to tell us: *"Well done, thou good and faithful servant: thou hast been faithful over a few things, I will make thee ruler over many things"* (Matthew 25:21).

Does God Trust You?

If you plan to be on the receiving end of God's wealth transfer, resist the temptation to become distracted or influenced by the personality of others. Stay pure and righteous before the Lord.

Let me offer this warning: do not get caught in the trap of being responsible for someone else's irresponsibility!

———— ∾ ————

Do not get caught in the trap of being responsible for someone else's irresponsibility!

You see, the minute God begins to pour out His blessings on you, the weak-minded will seek you out and attempt to latch themselves onto your success. If you are not careful, they will drain your energy and, like thieves, rob you of God's future for your life.

Oh, they'll arrive with smiles on their faces—and may shout "Hallelujah" and cry real tears. But pay attention to what Scripture says concerning such people. *"A man void of understanding striketh [shakes] hands, and becometh surety in the presence of his friend"* (Proverbs 17:18).

In other words, a man who cosigns a note for an acquaintance is foolish! In addition to the risk of not being paid back, this will disqualify you from being trusted by God. Why? Because you failed to use wisdom and did not pay attention to His Word.

The Bible also warns, *"Be not thou one of them that strike hands, or of them that are sureties for debts"* (Proverbs 22:26)—or helps people in debt.

This is Scripture, and it does not allow exceptions for family members!

Even more, *"He that is surety for a stranger shall smart for it"* (Proverbs 11:15). To "smart" means to "be broken or damaged"—they're going to break you!

Being entangled in these traps will hinder you from the flow of God's abundance.

Six Steps to Receiving God's Favor

The eyes of the Lord are searching across the earth for those who will be the beneficiaries of the outpouring He is planning. How can you be included? Let me share these six God-directed steps:

Step #1: Always see yourself as a work in progress.

To receive the Lord's favor, view yourself as a work under construction. Never conclude, "My task is complete."

In the parable of the rich fool, Jesus spoke of the man who thought he "had it made" and bragged, *"I will pull down my barns, and build greater; and there will I bestow all my fruits and my goods. And I will say to my soul, Soul, thou hast much goods laid up for many years; take thine ease, eat, drink, and be merry"* (Luke 12:18-19).

To this, the Lord responded, *"Thou fool, this night thy soul shall be required of thee: then whose shall those things be, which thou hast provided? So is he that layeth up treasure for himself, and is not rich toward God"* (verses 20-21).

38

Do not take early retirement from heaven's assignment, or you will exempt yourself from God's blessing.

———————— ∾ ————————

Do not take early retirement from heaven's assignment, or you will exempt yourself from God's blessing.

Scripture commands us, *"Occupy till I come"* (Luke 19:13).

Nowhere in the Bible does it say the Lord will bless your hands, rather, *"God shall bless...all the works of thine hands"* (Deuteronomy 16:15). The Lord values our labor.

Step #2: Be generous.

Are you praying for God to fill your cup to overflowing? Then be generous to others. For example, never pay someone less compensation than he or she deserves. The Almighty says, *"I will recompense them according to their deeds, and according to the works of their own hands"* (Jeremiah 25:14).

Here is God's opinion of those who refuse to pay proper wages:

Go to now, ye rich men, weep and howl for your miseries that shall come upon you. Your riches are corrupted, and your garments are motheaten, your gold and silver is cankered; and the rust of them shall be a witness against you, and shall eat your flesh as it were fire. Ye have heaped treasure together for the last days. Behold, the hire of the laborers who have reaped down your fields, which is of you kept back by fraud, crieth: and the cries of them which have reaped are entered into the ears of the Lord of sabaoth. (James 5:1-4)

An attitude of stinginess can erect a barrier which obstructs God's flow of blessings.

Step #3: Give to those in need.

It is the Father's plan for the storehouses of His children to be filled to capacity—and then some! But He fully expects for us to be compassionate and give to those less fortunate.

God takes a dim view of individuals who give for selfish reasons of prestige or the buying of favor.

———— ∽ ————

God takes a dim view of individuals who give for selfish reasons of prestige or the buying of favor.

Scripture declares, *"He that oppresseth the poor to increase his riches, and he that giveth to the rich, shall surely come to want"* (Proverbs 22:16).

Writing out a check to gain influence is against God's will. Not only will it backfire, but it may eliminate you from the blessed day of wealth transfer.

Here is a powerful verse you should commit to memory: *"He that giveth unto the poor shall not lack: but he that hideth his eyes shall have many a curse"* (Proverbs 28:27).

When God's Word speaks of the impoverished, it is not just referring to Christians living in poverty. No, you are to give to those in need regardless of their religion, color, or nationality.

You may ask, "Specifically, how does giving to the

needy qualify me for the wealth transfer God is preparing?"

Let me share a verse which clearly states this fact: *"He that by usury and unjust gain increaseth his substance, he shall gather it for him that will pity the poor"* (Proverbs 28:8).

What a promise! The Almighty will take the money from one who has amassed his fortune by charging exorbitant interest and give it to the person who has helped the downtrodden. Without question, it's a divine wealth transfer!

There is also a stern warning to the individual who turns a blind eye and extends an empty hand to those in need. Scripture cautions, *"Whoso stoppeth his ears at the cry of the poor, he also shall cry himself, but shall not be heard"* (Proverbs 21:13).

Every act of kindness is an investment in the treasury of heaven—and it will pay eternal dividends.

———— ⁓ ————

Every act of kindness is an investment in the treasury of heaven —and it will pay eternal dividends.

"He that hath pity upon the poor lends to the LORD, and that which he hath given he will pay him again" (Proverbs 19:17).

Hallelujah! You can never outgive God!

Step #4: Place your treasure in the vaults of heaven.

If your faith rests in God, His dwelling place is where you are to store your riches.

In the Sermon on the Mount, Jesus gives us these instructions: *"Lay not up for yourselves treasures upon earth, where moth and rust doth corrupt, and where thieves break through and steal: But lay up for yourselves treasures in heaven, where neither moth nor rust doth corrupt, and where thieves do not break through nor steal"* (Matthew 6:19-20).

Then the Lord makes this important statement: *"For where your treasure is, there will your heart be also"* (verse 21).

Indulging in selfish luxury is futile—especially since you can't take your possessions with you when you die. Your treasure must follow your heart.

Step #5: Sow bountifully.

It is a principle of the harvest that, *"He which soweth sparingly shall reap also sparingly; and he which soweth bountifully shall reap also bountifully"* (2 Corinthians 9:6).

We are also told, *"Every man according as he purposeth in his heart, so let him give; not grudgingly, or of necessity: for God loveth a cheerful giver. And God is able to make all grace abound toward you; that ye, always having all sufficiency in all things, may abound to every good work"* (verses 7-8).

This is the grace of financial blessing given to you as a present from God—not because of your own capabilities. And it is His grace which keeps this gift alive and brings continued blessings.

The word *abound* goes well beyond sufficiency. It means you will have more than you can ever use for your personal needs.

As you keep reading this passage you will find the most overlooked message in Scripture regarding the *reason* for our giving.

The Word tells us:

Now he that ministereth seed to the sower both minister bread for your food, and multiply your seed sown, and increase the fruits of your righteousness. Being enriched in every thing to all bountifulness, which causeth through us thanksgiving to God. For the administration of this service not only supplieth the want of the saints, but is abundant also by many thanksgivings unto God. Whiles by the experiment of this ministration they glorify God for your professed subjection unto the gospel of Christ." (verses 10-13)

God wants our giving to not only benefit the world, but most important, to bring souls to the foot of the cross.

The true giver is one who has subjected himself or herself unto the Gospel of Christ.

———— ∾ ————

The true giver is one who has subjected himself or herself unto the Gospel of Christ.

Please read this passage again and again until it is part of your spirit.

I often hear teaching on sowing and reaping which is not biblical because it deals with selfishness, not the Gospel. The body of Christ is being told, "If you give this, you will get that," yet the Bible says by our giving we profess our obedience to the Gospel.

The question rarely asked is, "What moves people to give to the Lord?" Are they simply doing so to personally receive?

When you take the cross out of "sowing and reaping," you have lost the heart of the harvest.

———— ~ ————

When you take the cross out of "sowing and reaping," you have lost the heart of the harvest.

Start giving for the Gospel's sake and watch what miracles the Lord will perform. You will prepare yourself for that glorious day when the most bountiful harvest in history will occur.

Step #6: Never stop giving.

If we expect to be a recipient of the coming wealth transfer, giving must become our daily lifestyle. As believers we are to regularly support the spreading of the Gospel (1 Corinthians 16:2).

Scripture records, "*There is that scattereth, and yet increaseth*" (Proverbs 11:24). When we freely give, God pours out even more!

Are you faithfully practicing the principles which result in God's amazing favor?

4

NO LACK!

God doesn't believe in just handing out the crumbs or leftovers from His table. He gives us this promise: *"And all these blessings shall come on thee, and overtake thee"* (Deuteronomy 28:2). Your life will be completely *covered* with His favor.

The blessings of God will flow to such an extent they will overpower you.

The Lord is certainly concerned about our everyday pressures—such as bills being paid. But what we are speaking of is far greater—a transfer of abundance in the *billions,* not millions.

To finance the end-time harvest will take a staggering amount of money, yet God has this and more in His storehouse.

If you are worried about your business or your household budget, these necessities will be taken care of and your family blessed. But God Almighty will go beyond your needs to fulfill heaven's vision for the entire earth.

While we prepare for this great and glorious moment, the Lord will multiply your seed today. How does He give to you? Through ideas, through sending you more clients or patients, through opening doors before you.

According to the Word, He will bless your farm even when there's famine in your neighbor's field.

———— ∾ ————

According to the Word, He will bless your farm even when there's famine in your neighbor's field.

The Invasion

During the reigns of David and Solomon there was so much wealth that silver was as common a commodity as stone (2 Chronicles 1:15).

Gold was in such abundance in the land that after their reigns, when Israel had departed from God and His Word, two mighty superpowers invaded the territory. Even more astonishing, it took the enemies four hundred years to carry the bounty out of the nation!

The looting began with the Assyrians, who raided again and again. Then it was Nebuchadnezzar's turn.

During the time of Israel's kings, when the people rebelled against God, foreign, heathen armies would attack. In some cases, Israel paid off the invaders just to get rid of them!

Whose money were they using? It was not only the gold brought from Egypt during the Exodus, but Solomon had ships which sailed to other kingdoms and returned with gold and precious commodities—and Israel became the envy of the world.

However, invasion after invasion eventually left the land desolate. Even the trees were plundered, and the country remained in a deplorable condition until it was restored by the return of the Jews in 1948.

"One Heart and One Soul"

At the time of Christ, Israel was under the domination of the Romans. And even though the nation was still poor, there were some Jews who had become prosperous, owning houses and property. Many of these people came to Christ when Peter and the disciples began to preach the Gospel after the Upper Room outpouring of the Holy Spirit. On one day alone *"there were added unto them about three thousand souls"* (Acts 2:41).

———— ∼ ————

On one day alone "there were added unto them about three thousand souls" (Acts 2:41).

There was something remarkable about these new converts. *"Neither was there any among them that lacked: for as many as were possessors of lands or houses sold them, and brought the prices of the things that were sold, and laid them down at the apostles' feet: and distribution was made unto every man according as he had need"* (Acts 4:34-35).

No lack!

You see, *"the multitude of them that believed were of one heart and of one soul: neither said any of them that ought of the things which he possessed was his own; but they had all things common"* (Acts 4:32).

All of this occurred because *"great power"* (verse 22) was evident and flowing in the early church.

There was such unity. Not one of them complained, "This is mine." Instead, they rejoiced, "It's God's!" And they were willing to forfeit everything they owned for the sake of the Gospel.

An Agenda for the Ages

Consider how much money it took to care and provide for these thousands of brand new believers. In today's economy it would amount to hundreds of millions of dollars.

It was not until AD 70 that the church was driven out of Jerusalem and forced to disperse throughout the world. So from the time of Jesus's ascension into heaven—over thirty-five years—these people prospered in Jerusalem.

This is one more example of what's about to happen again—but on a much grander scale. The day of this new outpouring is fast approaching. Your days of struggle are about to end as God fulfills His agenda for the ages.

———— ∼ ————

Your days of struggle are about to end as God fulfills His agenda for the ages.

The Folly of Deceit

Rebelling against what the Lord is doing is dangerous. In the same body of believers, where every need was being met, was a man named Ananias.

While his fellow Christians were selling their earthly goods to spread the Gospel, the Bible records how *"Ananias, with Sapphira his wife, sold a possession, and kept back part of the price, his wife also being privy to it, and brought a certain part, and laid it, at the apostles' feet"* (Acts 5:1-2).

Immediately, Peter said to Ananias, *"Why hath Satan filled thine heart to lie to the Holy Ghost, and to keep back part of the price of the land?"* (verse 3).

Because he tried to deceive the Holy Spirit, Ananias fell dead on the spot! (verse 5).

Three hours later, his wife Saphira returned and also lied regarding the price of the land. She, too, instantly fell dead.

It is a grave mistake to attempt to deceive the Holy Spirit.

It All Belongs to Him

As God begins to bless and prosper you, don't become carried away with your success and take your eyes off of the Source. Scripture makes this clear, *"Riches are not for ever"* (Proverbs 27:24). And we are asked, *"Doth the crown endure to every generation?"* (verse 24).

Everything in heaven and on earth belongs to God.

- *"The silver is mine, and the gold is mine, saith the LORD of hosts"* (Haggai 2:8).

- *"The earth is the LORD'S, and the fulness thereof"* (Psalm 24:1).

- *"Thine, O LORD, is the greatness, and the power, and the glory, and the victory, and the majesty: for all that is in the heaven and in the earth is thine; thine is the kingdom, O LORD, and thou art exalted as head above all"* (1 Chronicles 29:11).

- *"Both riches and honour come of thee, and thou reignest over all; and in thine hand is power and might; and in thine hand it is to make great, and to give strength unto all"* (1 Chronicles 29:12).

The Danger of Chasing Wealth

In an age where success and riches are almost worshiped, don't make a shrine of the money you've accumulated, because it can disappear like dust. The Bible gives this advice: *"Labour not to be rich: cease from thine own wisdom. Wilt thou set thine eyes upon that which is not? for riches certainly make themselves wings; they fly away as an eagle toward heaven"* (Proverbs 23:4-5).

As we learned in the story of Ananias and Saphira, chasing wealth can even cost you your life. God's Word declares, *"The ways of every one that is greedy of gain...taketh away the life of the owners thereof"* (Proverbs 1:19).

Instead of focusing on finances, we must keep *"looking unto Jesus the author and finisher of our faith"* (Hebrews 12:2).

When the Lord is your Provider, there will be no lack!

5

THE WEALTH OF
THE WICKED

During one of our partner conferences, a sincere gentleman approached me with this question: "Pastor, I know God wants me to prosper, but why does my next door neighbor who is not living for the Lord enjoy such wealth?"

This is not a new concern but an issue which has bothered believers since Old Testament times.

I pointed the man to a passage in God's Word which states, *"For the turning away of the simple shall slay them, and the prosperity of fools shall destroy them"* (Proverbs 1:32).

During our ministry, I have met many who wrestled with the same thoughts as this man. They were intelligent, godly, anointed individuals whom God was blessing. Yet, they lived on the same street with sinners who were twice as prosperous. It's only natural to ask, "Lord, why? I'm giving for the Gospel and he's living for the devil. It doesn't make any sense!"

———— ∼ ————

It's only natural to ask, "Lord, why? I'm giving for the Gospel and he's living for the devil. It doesn't make any sense!"

David's Envy

King David had the same concerns. He wrote, *"Truly God is good to Israel, even to such as are of a clean heart. But as for me, my feet were almost gone; my steps had well nigh slipped. For I was envious at the foolish, when I saw the prosperity of the wicked"* (Psalm 73:1-3).

He almost backslid over his jealousy of the wealthy because he saw them thriving, seemingly having no struggles, and their physical bodies were healthy and strong (verse 4). *"They are not in trouble as other men; neither are they plagued like other men"* (verse 5).

In addition, David observed how the wealthy were clothed with pride and *"their eyes stand out with fatness"* (verse 7). In other words, they have so much excess you can see it on their faces! And *"they have more than heart could wish"* (verse 7).

A Full Cup

What disturbed David the most was the fact these men were *"corrupt, and speak wickedly concerning oppression: they speak loftily. They set their mouth against the heavens, and their tongue walketh through the earth"* (Psalm 73:8-9).

He tells how the ungodly *"return hither: and waters of a full cup are wrung out to them"* (verse 10). For them there is no famine, and the rich man's family and friends are well taken care of. Feeling secure in their success, the sinner questions, "What does God have to do with any of this?" (verse 11).

David concludes his lament, *"Behold, these are the ungodly, who prosper in the world; they increase in riches"* (verse 12). Yet, these people are not giving to God.

Laden with Gold

I'm sure you've met such individuals. I certainly have—in fact some of my own cousins fit this description.

I was fourteen years old when our family left Israel and moved to Canada. My father had four brothers, and one of them became quite successful in the tire business.

At the time, there was a law in Israel that legislated you could not leave the country with more than ten thousand dollars. So my uncle invested his money in gold bracelets for his kids—thirteen in all. When they emigrated, those children were decked out in gold bracelets up and down both arms and around their necks!

———— ≈ ————

When they emigrated, those children were decked out in gold bracelets up and down both arms and around their necks!

In Toronto, this same uncle started a business where he would buy large quantities of merchandise from stores that were going into bankruptcy—then he would resell the products for a huge profit. And his children began doing the same.

To say he became wealthy is an understatement. He had vast warehouses around the city just to store the inventory.

I remember visiting one of his locations before he died. Only those in the trade could buy there, but I saw a unique lamp with a phone attached to it and asked, "Uncle, how much would you charge me for that?"

He paused for a moment and responded, "For you, Benny, twenty-five dollars."

I was excited and thought, "What a bargain!" and quickly shelled out the money.

Another cousin, watching, began to laugh at me. "What was so funny?" I later asked.

"I think you've been had!" he replied. "Your uncle paid about twenty-five cents for that thing!"

The Answer to the Dilemma

In David's day, he grew so upset seeing unbelievers prosper; he even thought that keeping his heart pure must be a waste of time (Psalm 73:13). And, *"When I thought to know this, it was too painful for me"* (verse 16).

However, in the house of the Lord, the Almighty gave David the answer. He wrote, *"I went into the sanctuary of God; then understood I their end. Surely thou didst set them in slippery places: thou castedst them down into destruction. How are they brought into desolation, as in a moment! they are utterly consumed with terrors"* (verses 17-19).

God is always in control—and in the end, the unrighteous will be left void and empty, while your life will be full.

———— ≈ ————

God is always in control—and in the end, the unrighteous will be left void and empty, while your life will be full.

Laid Up for the Righteous

Don't waste precious time and energy fretting over the riches of an unbeliever. One day the tables will be turned. God's Word declares:

Here is the fate God allots to the wicked, the heritage a ruthless man receives from the Almighty: However many his children, their fate is the sword; his offspring will never have enough to eat. The plague will bury those who survive him, and their widows will not weep for them. Though he heaps up silver like dust and clothes like piles of clay, what he lays up the righteous will wear, and the innocent will divide his silver. The house he builds is like a moth's cocoon, like a hut made by a watchman. He lies down wealthy, but will do so no more; when he opens his eyes, all is gone. Terrors overtake him like a flood; a tempest snatches him away in the night. The east wind carries him off, and he is gone; it sweeps him out of his place. It hurls itself against him without mercy as he flees headlong from its power. It claps its hands in derision and hisses him out of his place. (Job 27:13-23, NIV)

What an indictment!

God is telling us, "Let him go on building his empire, because the day is fast approaching when the righteous will wear his riches. And those who serve God will use it for His glory!"

That is why we need to redirect our energy and pray for our unsaved loved ones—so that the Lord will remove the blinders which cloud their vision so they can see clearly.

Scripture tells us, *"He that loveth silver shall not be satisfied with silver; nor he that loveth abundance with increase: this is also vanity. When goods increase, they are increased that eat them: and what good is there to the owners thereof, saving the beholding of them with their eyes?"* (Ecclesiastes 5:10-11).

They will lose everything they have accumulated and their riches will cause them pain (verse 13).

It's Yours!

Let me remind you again, God is reserving the wealth of this earth for those who have called upon His name. He is only allowing the wicked to use it temporarily in order to increase its value for you.

The Lord said to Israel, *"And I have given you a land for which ye did not labour, and cities which ye* built not, and ye dwell in them; of the vineyards and oliveyards which ye planted not do ye eat" (Joshua 24:13).

This transfer is on the way! *"A good man leaveth an inheritance to his children's children: and the wealth of the sinner is laid up for the just"* (Proverbs 13:22). God's abundance will affect not only you but your family, plus the offspring of your children.

———— ≈ ————

God's abundance will affect not only you but your family, plus the offspring of your children.

What I love about this promised gift is that it will be in our hands for as long as it takes to carry the Gospel to the nations.

Hidden Riches

I thank God that *"in the house of the righteous is much treasure"* (Proverbs 15:6). Even more *"there is treasure to be desired and oil in the dwelling of the* wise; but a foolish man spendeth it up" (Proverbs 21:20).

If you foolishly squander what the Lord has graciously given you, it will be forever gone. Avoid spending time on anything that will deplete your talents, your assets, your relationships, or your spiritual strength.

God is preparing your heart, soul, and mind for that glorious day. You see, He can't trust just anyone with what is about to occur, because they have wasted what has already been placed in their hands.

———— ∼ ————

God is preparing your heart, soul, and mind for that glorious day. You see, He can't trust just anyone with what is about to occur, because they have wasted what has already been placed in their hands.

The Lord makes this amazing pledge: *"I will go before thee, and make the crooked places straight: I will break in pieces the gates of brass, and cut in sunder the bars of iron: and I will give thee the treasures of darkness, and hidden riches of secret places, that thou mayest know that I, the LORD, which call thee by thy name, am the God of Israel"* (Isaiah 45:2-3).

Plant this powerful promise in your spirit.

A Vow of Oil

Scripture speaks of the vows we are to make to God—and when they are fulfilled, miracles will happen.

I was raised in a Greek Orthodox home in Israel yet didn't know much about the Bible.

In 1966 my father, who worked for the Israeli government, was told we could not leave the country for five years because of the sensitive information he had been privy to.

However, the next year, in June 1967, the Six-Day War broke out and things drastically changed.

I was only fourteen years old at the time but distinctly remember the trauma and tension pulsating in the nation. With childlike faith I prayed and made this vow to God: "If You will safely get us out of this country, I will give You a barrel of olive oil."

This may sound like a strange prayer, but in our Greek Orthodox church, olive oil was used to light the lamps, and I believed the Lord would be pleased with a gift so valuable.

A short time after this, a man from the Canadian embassy phoned my father to say, "Mr. Hinn, we've worked everything out—don't ask me how. All of your paperwork is in order, and you can leave whenever you are ready."

More than three years earlier than expected, our family left Israel.

My first job as a teenager in Canada was selling hot dogs at a little kiosk in the Fairview Mall in Toronto. And on a Saturday after my first paycheck, I walked into a grocery store and asked the manager, "Where can I find the olive oil? I need the largest jug you have."

If there had been a barrel full I would have bought it all!

Soon after, I proudly walked into the Greek Orthodox church and fulfilled the vow I had made to God in Jaffa. I placed the oil at the front of the altar and quietly said, "Thank You, Lord. Thank You for bringing us safely to our new home."

Your Divine Covenant

Vows to God are not to be made flippantly—and you may only make a few in your entire lifetime. They must be considered a serious matter between you and the Lord.

There are times in our Christian walk when we face a wall that can only be scaled by making a total commitment from your heart to the Almighty.

Today, don't be preoccupied with how others choose to live their life. When you make a divine covenant with the Lord, the riches of heaven will be yours.

6

Don't Look at the Clouds

Just a few short years ago, who would have believed the advances in communication and information technology we now take for granted. And I believe God is giving mankind brilliant, creative ideas for one reason—to fulfill Bible prophecy to preach the Gospel to the nations of the world.

God has shown me that He is going to place in our hands a new technology which will enable us to bring the message of redemption to every home on this earth.

I also believe He has placed you where you are at this moment in church history for His agenda to be fulfilled. As the apostle Paul wrote, *"God hath chosen the foolish things of the world to confound the wise; and God hath chosen the weak things of the world to confound the things which are mighty...and things which are not, to bring to nought things that are"* (1 Corinthians 1:27-28).

You Are Part of the Plan

We are on the verge of the greatest moment this side of eternity. It is the culmination of what began when Lucifer, one of the most beautiful and talented angels in heaven, rebelled against God and was thrown out of heaven.

We don't fully understand why, but the all-knowing Almighty knew this would happen. From the beginning, God had a plan—and you and I are a vital part of its fulfillment.

———— ∼ ————

From the beginning, God had a plan—and you and I are a vital part of its fulfillment.

74

One day soon our eyes will be opened and we will know what we do not comprehend today. And we'll praise Him for this knowledge eternally.

God knew a third of His holy angels would become His enemies (Revelation 12:3-4). He also had foreknowledge the earth would be destroyed by a flood, then restored—and that He would have to send His Son to die for humanity.

The Word declares, *"And he shall send Jesus Christ, which before was preached unto you: whom the heaven must receive until the times of restitution of all things, which God hath spoken by the mouth of all his holy prophets since the world began"* (Acts 3:20-21).

God also planned for His people and His church to be the tools He would use in the last days to bring all things to Himself. It is awesome to realize that we are part of God's end-time plan for the universe.

This is not a matter of good versus evil on earth; it is eternal. The Lord has ordained for us to be mightily used in this final act of restoration.

Ruling and Reigning

Almighty God has a remnant who will be trusted not only with the wealth of the nations, but with the authority God is about to give us eternally. This extends beyond a transfer of wealth. Praise God, we will rule and reign with Him forever!

Ruling with Him means that in heaven *"we shall judge angels"* (1 Corinthians 6:3).

This verse used to puzzle me until I realized angels were not created in the image and likeness of God as we are! As a result, they do not know His heart as we do.

In fact, the Bible says, *"Through the church, the manifold wisdom of God should be made known to the rulers and authorities in the heavenly realms"* (Ephesians 3:10, NIV). Think of it! The angels of heaven know God only by watching you and me, because they cannot know Him.

Jesus declared, *"But ye know him; for he dwelleth with you, and shall be in you"* (John 14:17).

The revelation of God comes to us directly through

Christ, who explained, *"All things are delivered unto me of my Father: and no man knoweth the Son, but the Father; neither knoweth any man the Father, save the Son, and he to whomsoever the Son will reveal him"* (Matthew 11:27).

The redeemed have been invited to a special dinner with the Lord (Revelation 3:20). As Jesus told the disciples at the Last Supper, *"I will not drink henceforth of this fruit of the vine, until that day when I drink it new with you in my Father's kingdom"* (Matthew 26:29).

Your Place of Authority

I pray you will begin to see beyond the realm of this present day and catch a glimpse of the glory God has planned.

———— ∽ ————

I pray you will begin to see beyond the realm of this present day and catch a glimpse of the glory God has planned.

The Bible says, *"Beloved, now are we the sons of God, and it doth not yet appear what we shall be: but we know that, when he shall appear, we shall be like him; for we shall see him as he is"* (1 John 3:2).

We have been chosen to take our place of authority in heaven. As Scripture tells us, *"To him that overcometh will I grant to sit with me in my throne"* (Revelation 3:21).

What gives us this right? It has been ordained by God. *"For if we be dead with him, we shall also live with him: If we suffer, we shall also reign with him"* (2 Timothy 2:11-12).

Because our human minds are limited, we may not fully understand what is about to transpire. But as Jesus proclaims, *"At that day ye shall know that I am in my Father, and ye in me, and I in you"* (John 14:20).

We will be one with Him.

Sow Abundantly

In preparation for our eternal destiny, God has placed us in a training camp here on earth.

Our living and *giving* is in expectation of the Lord's promises. The Bible teaches, *"Cast thy bread upon the waters: for thou shalt find it after many days. Give a portion to seven, and also to eight; for thou knowest not what evil shall be upon the earth"* (Ecclesiastes 11:1-2).

This command gives us an insight into God's mind. He teaches, "Don't only give once or twice—but many times." A farmer doesn't place one solitary seed into the ground when he plants, he sows *multiple* seeds.

———— ∾ ————

A farmer doesn't place one solitary seed into the ground when he plants, he sows multiple *seeds.*

In that passage the Lord gives us a reason for abundant sowing—because we do not know what evil lurks on the earth. This tells me my giving to God not only qualifies me for the day of transfer, but it also protects me from disaster!

Scripture also explains, *"If the clouds be full of rain, they empty themselves upon the earth: and if the tree* fall toward the south, or toward the north, in the place where the tree falleth, there it shall be" (verse 3).

In simple terms, conditions and circumstances will fluctuate and change, but "he that observeth the wind shall not sow; and he that regardeth the clouds shall not reap" (verse 4).

Stop worrying over the negative forces around you. It may be rainy or dry, windy or calm, but if you allow these factors to affect your sowing, you will lose God's blessings and protection for tomorrow.

Total Faith

The Lord is warning believers to wake up and start preparing for what is ahead. Jesus even lamented that "the children of this world are in their generation wiser than the children of light" (Luke 16:8). And we are also told, "As thou knowest not what is the way of the spirit, nor how the bones do grow in the womb of her that is with child: even so thou knowest not the works of God who maketh all" (Ecclesiastes 11:5).

We may not know how the Almighty operates, yet we can trust Him. Stop taking your cues from threatening clouds or howling winds.

When you truly believe God is in control, you will start sowing with total faith: *"In the morning sow thy seed, and in the evening withhold not thine hand: for thou knowest not whether shall prosper, either this or that, or whether they both shall be alike good"* (verse 6).

Don't Run from the Promise

When a devastating famine struck the land during the time of Isaac, the first thing he wanted to do was head for greener pastures in Egypt, where perhaps he could borrow money from a bank to start over.

My friend, problems will find you. There will always be recessions, depressions, and economic hardships.

———— ∽ ————

My friend, problems will find you.
There will always be recessions, depressions,
and economic hardships.

Isaac was about to follow the way of the world because it seemed the natural way out. He said, "Let's seek counsel from others and see if they can help."

But God commands, "No, I'm demanding that you live by faith."

There are certain things the Lord will allow us to seek advice for, but when it comes to sowing and reaping and our spiritual walk, we cannot rely on man.

God told Isaac, *"Go not down into Egypt"* (Genesis 26:2), but he was to stay in the land which was promised to him.

Isaac argued, "Lord, there's a famine here. I can't sow my seed."

God replied, "You are wrong. Success is not dependent on the conditions around you."

The Turnaround

Change is urgently required. It is time to have *"the mind of Christ"* (1 Corinthians 2:16) and begin thinking like the Father.

- The world believes that what is strong will become weak. God says what is weak will become strong (2 Corinthians 12:10).

- The world believes that what is full will be empty. God says what's empty will be full (2 Kings 4:3-6).
- The world believes that what is alive will die. God says, no, only the dead will live (Romans 6:11).

A Hundredfold Blessing!

Armed with nothing more than faith, trust, and obedience to God, Isaac took his seed and planted in the parched earth—and watched a miracle unfold.

The Bible records, *"Then Isaac sowed in that land, and received in the same year an hundredfold: and the LORD blessed him"* (Genesis 26:12).

In a time of desolation, he prospered: *"And the man waxed great, and went forward, and grew until he became very great: For he had possession of flocks, and possession of herds, and great store of servants"* (verses 13-14).

You can imagine what happened when his fellow landowners saw his fortune blossom before their eyes. Scripture says, *"The Philistines envied him"* (verse 14).

The difference between Isaac and the world is that he believed God and sowed in a dry, arid land.

Today, the Lord is asking you to be moved by faith rather than reason, by hope instead of fear, by obedience rather than doubt.

Get ready! His glorious rain of abundance is about to fall on you!

7

SOW YOUR WAY OUT OF A CRISIS

The year was 1979 and I was in Orlando, Florida, in the home of Roy Harthern, preparing to marry his beautiful daughter, Suzanne.

It was one of those times when a future father-in-law was getting to know more about a young man who would soon be a member of the family. He was seated on the floor of his living room, right next to the fireplace.

We discussed a variety of topics—how I was raised, my brothers and sisters, and my travels to various countries of the world.

However, since both of us were in ministry and I

had preached in his church, most of our conversation focused on the work of the Lord.

Then, out of the blue, Roy asked me a question which nearly floored me: "Tell me about your giving."

"What do your mean?" I wanted to know.

"Well," he continued, "how much do you give to the Lord's work? I want to know the amounts. How much?"

"My giving is between me and God," I countered, feeling quite uncomfortable sharing such personal information.

---— ∼ —---

"My giving is between me and God," I countered, feeling quite uncomfortable sharing such personal information.

Not satisfied with my answer, he insisted, "I'm going to be your father-in-law, so it's really about God, you, and me. Let's talk."

An Emotional Giver?

Roy Harthern was born in England and I thought, for a conservative British man, he really is pushy.

But I responded in the best way I could, telling him the dollar amounts of what I had given the past Sunday, the Sunday before that, and as far back as I could remember. Some of the amounts were large, some average, and some small, depending on my circumstances and finances at the time.

"Well now," he said, "I've been sitting here racking my brain wondering why a young man like you—being so successful in your healing meetings—is in debt." And he added, "Now I know why."

Curious, I asked, "Tell me."

"You are an emotional giver," he concluded. Then he asked, "How would you like for God to give to you the way you've been giving to Him? One day you give more, one day you give less. Up and down, up and down. If you feel good, you give more. If you feel bad, you give less. What would you think if the Lord treated you in the same manner?"

"Repay God—with Interest!"

Then Pastor Harthern made a statement that still rings in my ears to this day. "Benny," he said, "never forget this as long as you live. The law of giving is a fixed law you cannot change."

Then he took out his Bible and said, "God's Word declares you must give to His work. This is more than just friendly advice; He gave you a command."

Next, he asked, "How long have you been saved?"

"Since February 1972," I answered.

"Benny," he added, "you owe God 20 percent for every year."

"What do you mean?" I wanted to know.

He said, "You owe God more money than you owe the world. And you are to go back—starting with the day of your salvation—and repay the Lord everything you owe Him, with 20 percent interest." Then he added, "Unless you correct this with God, you'll never recover from your debt."

At that moment my emotions were all over the place—I was trembling, scared, and angry. Yet I knew he was right. I also thought of the interest charged by banks and credit card companies, and it was often more than what we consider a tithe.

Was This God?

Flying back to Toronto on Eastern Airlines there was a battle raging inside of me. I thought, Do I do this, or not? Is this God, or isn't it? Do I really obey Roy Harthern, or should I forget what he said?

At the time we had a little less than ten thousand dollars in our ministry account, but what we owed was much, much more. However, I came to the conclusion that my future father-in-law was right. I had nothing to lose—since we were already sinking deep in debt and were about to be sued for the cancellation of a Holy Land tour. Our young ministry was on the verge of bankruptcy. I thought, there's only one way to go—and that is up!

———— ∾ ————

I thought, there's only one way to go—and that is up!

The words of Pastor Harthern were foremost in my mind. "Your way out of debt is to give to God."

Get out the Checkbook

I drove over to our small ministry office and said to our secretary, Marion Robinson, "I have a job for you."

"What do you need?" responded this dear woman who truly loved the Lord. She was in her sixties and I was in my twenties. We called her "One Finger Marion" because even though she had ten good fingers, she only typed with one!

"Get out the checkbook," I asked. We are going to send out several one-thousand-dollar checks. Make the first one out to World Vision." Then I started naming a list of ministries who would receive similar checks.

Without my knowing, Marion went to a phone and made emergency calls to the members of our board—and before long all nine of them showed up at the office.

Gone Crazy?

"What are you doing?" they wanted to know. "Why are you spending this money when we have all these obligations? Have you gone crazy?"

"God wants me to," I answered. "I owe the Lord far more than I owe these people."

"But you can't do that," they replied, "We'll have to close down the ministry."

One board member exclaimed, "I can't have any part of this. You have to pay your bills. That's just the way it is!"

———— ≈ ————

One board member exclaimed, "I can't have any part of this. You have to pay your bills. That's just the way it is!"

"Gentlemen," I told them, "with what we have in the bank we can pay maybe one or two of our debts and that's all. A few days from now we will probably be screamed at by the rest. But the one I really owe is God—He is more important than all of them combined!"

An Empty Account

Seven of the board members resigned on the spot—and, in disbelief, walked out of the meeting.

91

Two men—Fred Spring and Fred Brown, God bless them—stuck around. I'll never forget dear Fred Brown. He was trembling and his lower lip was shaking as he asked, "Benny, are you sure you know this is God?"

"Yes," I replied, "As certain as anything in this world."

"Then I'm sticking with you," he said.

Marion began typing with her finger—one check at a time. By that afternoon the account was empty and the checks were in the mail.

Inside, I was praying, "Lord, I'm doing what You and Roy Harthern said, Now let's see what happens."

———— ∽ ————

Inside, I was praying, "Lord, I'm doing what You and Roy Harthern said, Now let's see what happens."

My Last Dime

The next Sunday I drove to Evangel Temple in my Pontiac, white with the bright red top. Financially, I was at the bottom of the barrel, with ten cents in my pocket—the only money I had in this world.

When it was time for the offering, I said to myself, "Lord, you know I've already given," and I began clutching my last dime, thinking, "No way am I going to let this go."

When the usher reached my row, he began to pass the red plate lined with gold trim—I can still see it. I was seated near the end of the aisle, and for some reason the man held the plate right in front of me and didn't move.

In this awkward moment, I said to myself, "Lord, You can't be serious!"

My hand was shaking as I pulled that lonely dime out of my pocket, but my fingers didn't want to let go.

Finally, the ten cents dropped into the offering plate, and it seemed as if my whole life fell with it.

For the first time, I was at absolute zero!

In the Psalms, David spoke of sowing in tears (Psalm 126:5). That was me. My entire being was crying out, "My God, I can't believe I just did this."

My Treat

On Sundays I used to go with friends to a restaurant called the Swiss Chalet—they had the best chicken in town. It was my custom to pay for my lunch and treat someone else.

This day, however, I had nothing and looked for excuses not to go. At that very moment, a friend walked up to me and asked, "Are you going with us to the Swiss Chalet? This time it's my treat!"

After lunch I went home and said to myself, "This is it! Tomorrow we declare bankruptcy."

Shocked!

The next day, when I walked into the office, there was a letter from a Canadian evangelist who didn't particularly care for our ministry. When I saw his name on the top of the envelope, I cringed, "Oh my, he's going to tell me off again."

I recalled the time this man walked up to me in a downtown Toronto hotel and actually said, right to my face, "I don't like you—and I pray you will fail. You're a threat to our ministry." I could hardly believe the words I was hearing from this evangelist.

When I opened the letter, however, I was absolutely shocked. Inside was a check for a thousand dollars with a note: "God told me today to send this to you."

———— ∽ ————

Inside was a check for a thousand dollars with a note: "God told me today to send this to you."

I looked at the postmark and it was the exact same day we sent out our checks—and the Lord clearly directed me to send one of them to this evangelist's ministry. Our checks crossed in the mail!

Today, he and I are friends, and I later learned that at that particular time his ministry was struggling through dire financial problems as we were. Yet, God directed him to sow his last seed.

Shouting and Dancing

Over the next few days we experienced a week of absolute miracles. I'll never forget it as long as I live.

Money began pouring in from people we had never heard from before.

There were notes attached to the checks saying, "God woke me up last night and told me to send this to you." And, "I feel impressed of the Lord to help your ministry at this time."

I was literally shouting and dancing around the office as we excitedly opened the mail. "Marion, look! This giving really works! It really does!"

"Shall we call the board?" she asked.

"No," I replied, "those who left made their decision. We're moving forward without them."

Within a few months every debt we owed was paid, our legal problems were solved, and we had a surplus in the ministry account.

Reaping in Joy

It took parting with my last dime for the Lord to prove to me that we can sow our way out of a crisis. Praise God!

Now I understood the rest of what David wrote concerning proving God with our giving: *"They that sow in tears shall reap in joy. He that goeth forth and weepeth, bearing precious seed, shall doubtless come again with rejoicing, bringing his sheaves with him"* (Psalm 126:5-6). This is not a matter of luck or coincidence; it is the result of obedience.

———— ∾ ————

This is not a matter of luck or coincidence; it is the result of obedience.

A Morsel of Bread

During the ministry of the prophet Elijah, the word of the Lord came to him at a dried-up brook called Cherith, saying, *"Arise, get thee to Zarephath...and dwell there: behold, I have commanded a widow woman there to sustain thee"* (1 Kings 17:9).

When he arrived at the gate of the city, he saw a woman who was gathering sticks. Thirsty, Elijah called out to her, *"Fetch me, I pray thee, a little water in a vessel, that I may drink"* (verse 10).

As she went to draw some water, the prophet also requested, *"Bring me, I pray thee, a morsel of bread in thine hand"* (verse 11).

The Meal Multiplied

The woman's predicament was desperate. She said to Elijah, *"As the LORD thy God liveth, I have not a cake, but an handful of meal in a barrel, and a little oil in a cruse: and, behold, I am gathering two sticks, that I may go in and dress it for me and my son, that we may eat it, and die"* (1 Kings 17:12).

Elijah told her not to worry, "Go ahead and do what you have planned, but make me a little cake first—then some for you and your son."

She replied, "You don't understand. I do not have enough for all of us."

Elijah continued, *"For thus saith the LORD God of Israel, The barrel of meal shall not waste, neither shall the cruse of oil fail, until the day that the LORD sendeth rain upon the earth"* (verse 14).

Whether she believed this or not, the prophet was persistent, and I can see her picking up those sticks to light a fire and bake a little nourishment for him.

The Bible records, *"She went and did according to the saying of Elijah: and she, and he, and her house, did eat many days"* (verse 15). One version translates it "for a whole year."

What was supposed to be "one breakfast and then we are going to die" resulted in twelve months of food!

——— ~ ———

What was supposed to be "one breakfast and then we are going to die" resulted in twelve months of food!

Time to Sow

Are you willing to sacrifice your last seed? If so, God will qualify you for an outpouring of abundance.

Scripture declares, *"Behold that which I have seen: it is good and comely for one to eat and to drink, and to enjoy the good of all his labour that he taketh under the sun all the days of his life, which God giveth him: for it is his portion"* (Ecclesiastes 5:18).

Almighty God has ordained to give you all you need in life—food, clothing, a roof over your head, and enough money to sustain you and your family. But more than this, *"Every man also to whom God hath given riches and wealth, and hath given him power to eat thereof, and to take his portion, and to rejoice in his labour; this is the gift of God"* (verse 19).

The mountain you face may seem higher than you could ever climb. And, like a vise, the pressures of life may be squeezing you from all sides.

Regardless of your situation, when God says it is time to plant, follow His leading—even if it is the last seed you possess.

On the authority of God's Word and from personal experience, I can assure you there is a miracle ahead. Yes, you can sow your way out of a crisis.

8

OPENING THE
DOOR TO
A MIRACLE

One of the most fascinating stories in the Old Testament concerns Jacob and Esau—the twin sons of Isaac. Esau was actually born first but later sold his birthright to his brother, who used it to obtain his father's blessing before Isaac died.

This account is important for a number of reasons, including how a vow which includes our finances can transform the future.

The conflict between the two brothers intensified and reached the boiling point. The Bible records, *"Esau hated Jacob because of the blessing wherewith his father blessed him: and Esau said in his heart, The days of mourning for my father are at hand; then will I slay my brother Jacob"* (Genesis 27:41).

Rebekah, the mother of the two, told Jacob to journey to a place called Haran and spend time with Laban, her brother, until things calmed down—then she would send for him.

This was an adventure into the unknown. Jacob had never before met Laban and had no idea what he looked like. There were no convenient cell phones to call ahead and say, "Hey I'm coming to see you!" He didn't even have the man's address—just a general idea of where his uncle lived.

———— ≈ ————

There were no convenient cell phones to call ahead and say, "Hey I'm coming to see you!" He didn't even have the man's address—just a general idea of where his uncle lived.

On the other hand, Laban had no knowledge that one of his sister's sons was on his way for an extended visit.

Jacob's Ladder

While walking to this distant land, he stopped one night to sleep under the stars—using a stone for his pillow. There, in a dream, Jacob saw *"a ladder set up on the earth, and the top of it reached to heaven: and behold the angels of God ascending and descending on it"* (Genesis 28:12).

As the dream continued, he saw God standing above the ladder saying, *"I am the LORD God of Abraham thy father, and the God of Isaac: the land whereon thou liest, to thee will I give it, and to thy seed; and thy seed shall be as the dust of the earth, and thou shalt spread abroad to the west, and to the east, and to the north, and to the south: and in thee and in thy seed shall all the families of the earth be blessed"* (verses 13-14).

God also promised to be with Jacob and bring him back to his home: *"For I will not leave thee, until I have done that which I have spoken to thee of"* (verse 15).

When he awoke, Jacob knew this was a sacred place. So he took the stone which had been his pillow and set it up as a pillar, poured oil over it *"and he called the name of that place Bethel"* (verse 19).

He "Vowed a Vow"

That same morning, Jacob made a solemn covenant with the Almighty. Scripture states, *"And Jacob vowed a vow, saying, If God will be with me, and will keep me in this way that I go"* (Genesis 28:20).

He really wasn't sure of the future. That is why Jacob asked the Lord to keep him alive and protected while traveling. You see, he was on a journey from the Holy Land to what is now known as Iraq. This was a long distance which took many weeks, and there were dangers along the way.

Jacob also asked the Lord, *"Give me bread to eat, and raiment to put on"* (verse 20). He had no idea how he was going find the nourishment or clothing to sustain him.

His final request was *"that I come again to my father's house in peace"* (verse 21).

A Commitment to Tithe

Jacob made a sacrificial vow that if God would do these things—be with him, keep him safe, give him food, clothing, and bring him home again in peace —here is what he would do in return: *"Then shall the LORD be my God: and this stone, which I have set for a pillar, shall be God's house: and of all that thou shalt give me I will surely give the tenth unto thee"* (verses 21-22).

Jacob promised not only to build the Lord a place of worship, but also to tithe. He had known about giving God "a tenth of all" from his father, Isaac, and his father's father, Abraham, the first person in the Bible to tithe (Genesis 14:20).

Jacob's vow of tithing began that very day—putting aside 10 percent of everything he earned for the Lord.

———— ∼ ————

Jacob's vow of tithing began that very day—putting aside 10 percent of everything he earned for the Lord.

Peace in the Household

About twenty years later, when it was time for Jacob to return home, the Lord reminded him of the vow he had made: *"I am the God of Bethel, where thou anointedst the pillar, and where thou vowedst a vow unto me: now arise, get thee out from this land, and return unto the land of thy kindred"* (Genesis 31:13).

The most important detail of this statement is that God heard Jacob's vow. Heaven pays close attention when we make a covenant with the Almighty.

———— ∼ ————

Heaven pays close attention when we make a covenant with the Almighty.

Most people who read the Bible forget it was Jacob who built a sanctuary at Bethel—a place of worship and leadership used later by Samuel (1 Samuel 7:16).

Because of Jacob's faithfulness, when he arrived home, *"Esau ran to meet him, and embraced him, and fell on his neck, and kissed him: and they wept"* (Genesis 33:4).

Both God and Jacob kept the covenant, and there was harmony in the household once more.

"That's All I Need to Know"

Starting in those early days—and continuing to the present—a vow made between two people in the East is stronger than a contract made in the West.

When I was growing up in Israel it was rare for people to rely on written agreements. In my father's day, your word was your bond.

In fact, there are many portions of Scripture which talk about verbal pacts involving two parties—whether between two men or between man and God.

As an example, during a time when Israel rebelled against the Lord and came under the domination of the Philistines, Ammonites, and other heathen rule, the Lord raised up a Jewish man named Jephthah.

In the natural, Jephthah couldn't see any way out from the stranglehold of the enemy. He said, "Lord, I don't have the kind of power and experience to defeat these foes. I'm just a young man who loves You."

God replied, "That all I need to know."

An Irrevocable Pledge

To stave off an invasion, Jephthah sent the king of Ammon a message saying, *"I have not sinned against thee, but thou doest me wrong to war against me: the LORD the Judge be judge this day between the children of Israel and the children of Ammon"* (Judges 11:27).

The ruler, however, ignored his words.

At this point, Scripture describes how *"the Spirit of the LORD came upon Jephthah, and he passed over Gilead, and Manasseh, and passed over Mizpeh...unto the children of Ammon. And Jephthah vowed a vow unto the LORD, and said, If thou shalt without fail deliver the children of Ammon into mine hands, then it shall be, that whatsoever cometh forth of the doors of my house to meet me, when I return in peace from the children of Ammon, shall surely be the LORD'S, and I will offer it up for a burnt offering"* (verses 29-31).

With only a small army and the anointing of the Lord, Jephthah crossed from Israel into Jordan to face the fierce fighting men of Ammon. His vow was irrevocable: "If you give us victory, whatever comes out of my house when I return, I will offer that as a sacrifice to You."

By a miracle, God delivered the enemy, and the inhabitants *"of Ammon were subdued before the children of Israel"* (verse 33).

The Daughter Understood

Then came the shock of Jephthah's life. When he finally reached his home *"behold, his daughter came out to meet him with timbrels and with dances: and she was his only child"* (Judges 11:34).

Remembering his vow, when he saw her, Jephthah tore his clothes and cried, *"Alas, my daughter! thou hast brought me very low...for I have opened my mouth unto the LORD, and I cannot go back"* (verse 35).

This man realized what we also must know: if you make a vow to God, you'd better keep it!

———— ∾ ————

This man realized what we also must know: if you make a vow to God, you'd better keep it!

109

Even his precious child knew the price of this commitment. The daughter said to her father, *"If thou hast opened thy mouth unto the LORD, do to me according to that which hath proceeded out of thy mouth; forasmuch as the LORD hath taken vengeance for thee of thine enemies, even of the children of Ammon"* (verse 36).

Then she added, *"Let this thing be done for me: let me alone two months, that I may go up and down upon the mountains, and bewail my virginity"* (verse 37).

Did She Die?

Some Bible teachers believe Jephthah did not sacrifice his daughter but just kept her as a single woman for the rest of her life. They conclude this from the next verse, which reads, *"And he sent her away for two months: and she went with her companions, and bewailed her virginity upon the mountains"* (Judges 11:38).

Then we learn, *"And it came to pass at the end of two months, that she returned unto her father, who did with her according to his vow which he had vowed: and she knew no man"* (verse 39).

However, this is not the end of the story. Scripture records, *"And it was a custom in Israel, that the daughters of Israel went yearly to lament the daughter of Jephthah"* (verses 39-40).

Of course, she died. Having lived in that part of the world, I know the culture, and they certainly would not mourn someone who was alive. And you don't sorrow over a single person because she didn't marry. In fact, many women stayed single to serve God and were not lamented.

The only conclusion I can draw is that her father fulfilled his pledge to the Almighty.

So here was a man whose vow to God was so strong he would not go back on his word, regardless. He said, "I've made a covenant and I will not break it!"

The heart of the Lord must fill with sorrow when people make casual promises to Him and fail to keep them.

———— ∼ ————

The heart of the Lord must fill with sorrow when people make casual promises to Him and fail to keep them.

Do they not realize the danger in which they are placing themselves?

The Lord Remembered

You may be facing an impossible situation, but an agreement with God can change your destiny.

The Bible tells us of a man named Elkanah who had two wives, Peninnah and Hannah. The first bore him children, but Hannah remained barren.

Each year when Elkanah and his family went to Shiloh to offer sacrifices, he gave Hannah extra portions of the sacrificial meal *"for he loved Hannah: but the LORD had shut up her womb"* (1 Samuel 1:5). The rival wife, Peninnah, *"provoked her...to make her fret"* (verse 6). As a result, Hanna suffered unbearable shame.

One evening in Shiloh, she went to the tabernacle to pray concerning her plight, *"And she vowed a vow, and said, O LORD of hosts, if thou wilt indeed look on the affliction of thine handmaid, and remember me, and not forget thine handmaid, but wilt give unto thine handmaid a man child, then I will give him unto* the LORD *all the days of his life, and there shall no razor come upon his head"* (verse 11).

To show you the power of a commitment to God, when they returned home, Elkanah had intimate relations with Hannah *"and the LORD remembered her"* (verse 19).

What did God remember? Her vow!

———— ∾ ————

What did God remember? Her vow!

As Scripture records, *"Wherefore it came to pass, when the time was come about after Hannah had conceived, that she bare a son, and called his name Samuel, saying, Because I have asked him of the LORD"* (verse 20).

Your Vow Brings Victory

After Samuel was weaned, Hannah took him to the temple and presented her son to the high priest, Eli, saying, *"For this child I prayed; and the LORD hath given me my petition which I asked of him: therefore also I have lent him to the LORD; as long as he liveth he shall be lent to the LORD"* (1 Samuel 1:27-28).

Without Hannah's vow, there would have been no Samuel, one of the great prophets and leaders of Israel.

Jacob, Jephthah, and Hannah all learned that when you make and keep a vow to God, you open the door to a miracle.

9

THE
TURNAROUND

For two years in our ministry, I fought a battle where there seemed to be no answer. It was the most difficult trial we ever faced.

The circumstances involved a man who was determined to destroy everything we had worked and prayed for. He even went to authorities, accusing us of all sorts of misdeeds. As a result, officials came and examined many aspects of our organization, searching under every stone.

Even though we knew there was nothing wrong, the process itself drained our energies beyond measure and it was taking a toll on my physical health. I prayed, "Lord, when will this conflict end?"

After nearly twenty-four months of unrelenting pressure, while in Jerusalem, I deliberately took the time to go to what is known as the Wailing Wall. It is part of the Temple Mount and one of the most sacred places in all of Judaism.

Every day, the faithful come to pray, leaving their written petitions wedged between the stones of the ancient wall, some of which date back to the Second Temple in 500 BC.

My Bargain with God

In this hallowed place, I spoke with the Lord concerning the matter which was tearing at the very heart of our ministry. I looked up to heaven and made a vow to Almighty God: "Lord, if you will solve this problem, I will present to You the largest gift we have ever given to children who are in need"—and I named the amount.

I was desperate for an answer and, from the depth of my being, meant every word of my pledge to the Lord.

That day, as I walked way from the Wailing Wall, there was a peace that washed over me that is impossible to describe—even though all hell was breaking loose around me.

I didn't know how God would solve this onslaught, but I knew somehow He would.

――――――― ∼ ―――――――

I didn't know how God would solve this onslaught, but I knew somehow He would.

A Man Named Nabal

From Jerusalem, we flew to Kenya for a crusade. There, in my Nairobi hotel room, I opened my Bible to the book of 1 Samuel and began reading how David, after Samuel died, went out into the back country where a wicked man named Nabal lived. The man owned thousands of sheep and goats, and David and his men voluntarily guarded and protected the animals of this ungodly man.

It was sheep-shearing season and David instructed his men to approach Nabal in peace and ask him to be generous and share the feast.

Nabal indignantly answered David's servants by asking, *"Who is David? and who is the son of Jesse? there be many servants now a days that break away*

117

every man from his master. Shall I then take my bread, and my water, and my flesh that I have killed for my shearers, and give it unto men, whom I know not whence they be?" (1 Samuel 25:10-11).

As you continue reading, you learn the fate Nabal suffered for not honoring a servant of the Lord with bread. Scripture tells us how, after enjoying a huge banquet, his *"heart failed him and he became like a stone. About ten days later, the LORD struck Nabal and he died"* (verses 37-38, NIV).

When David heard of Nabal's death, he proclaimed, *"Praise be to the LORD, who has upheld my cause against Nabal for treating me with contempt. He has kept his servant from doing wrong and has brought Nabal's wrongdoing down on his own head"* (verse 39, NIV).

What a turnaround!

"Lord, Deliver Me"

When I read those words in Nairobi, I told the Lord, "I'm not sure I understand You very well. You took Nabal's life for not giving bread and water to

David, but you keep the man alive who is out to destroy Your work."

Then I repeated the vow I made previously in Jerusalem and said, "Lord, deliver me from this. I don't care how You do it, but lift this burden from our ministry."

A Shocking Announcement!

The next week I was back in the United States meeting with a group of attorneys because I had been requested to give a deposition in the legal case the man had filed against us.

When my wife, Suzanne, and I walked in the room, the lawyers were seated in front of us. One of them turned around and made a statement I could hardly believe. "He's dead," announced the attorney. "There isn't going to be any case."

"What are you talking about?" I asked.

"This morning, he died of a heart attack," said the counsel. The man had dropped dead on his way to an auction in the city where he lived.

Suzanne and I were in absolute shock—especially since he was a relatively young man.

It was the David and Nabal story all over again.

————— ∾ —————

It was the David and Nabal story all over again.

When I made my vow to God at the Wailing Wall, I had no idea how the Lord was going to solve the problem, but He did!

Now it was my turn. Immediately, we embarked on the most ambitious program of support for needy children in the history of our ministry. The burden was lifted and the Lord protected His Word.

The Way Out of Trouble

I want you to understand the power of a vow because the coming wealth transfer will be placed into the hands of those the Lord can trust—and He will honor a committed heart.

God does not take your intentions casually. He hears every word you speak and watches every action you take. That's why, if I ask God to deliver me and promise to support those in need, I had better keep my half of the agreement.

David made this powerful statement: *"I will go into thy house with burnt offerings: I will pay thee my vows, which my lips have uttered, and my mouth hath spoken, when I was in trouble"* (Psalm 66:13-14).

Sadly, many who are mired in problems, make outlandish promises to God: "If you'll just get me out of this mess, I'll start paying my tithes every week."

Then, when the storm clouds pass, they fail not only to give God what belongs to Him, but even to attend church!

A "Now" Answer

If you want to see God move on your behalf immediately, attach your giving to a vow. Let me share this proven truth. You can bring an offering and not see a harvest for ten years, but give a vow and you can see the results in a matter of days!

In less than three weeks from the time I prayed at the wall in Jerusalem, God completely solved the attack against our ministry—and in a manner which is still amazing to me.

If you desire a quick harvest, make a vow. Heaven will be activated and the Lord will begin to swiftly move in your situation.

The Lesson of Absalom

One of the most startling discoveries you'll ever make is how important God considers vows. He will even honor one from a person who is not righteous!

You may ask, "Is that possible?"

Let me share the account of Absalom, the third son of David, who was far from being an honorable man. He murdered his own brother, Amnon for sexually abusing their sister Tamar. Then he fled.

While he was away, however, Absalom made a vow to God: *"And it came to pass after forty years, that Absalom said unto the king, I pray thee, let me go and pay my vow, which I have vowed unto the LORD, in Hebron. For thy servant vowed a vow while I abode at Geshur in Syria, saying, If the LORD shall bring me again indeed to Jerusalem, then I will serve the LORD"* (2 Samuel 15:7-8).

The pact with God was straightforward: "If You let me return home, I will serve and worship You."

Broken Promises

Without question, the Almighty kept His part of the bargain. The Bible tells us how the Lord used Joab, the nephew of King David and the captain of his army, to bring Absalom back to Jerusalem. So the Lord *did* answer his prayer.

However, Absalom made the foolish decision to rebel against God and began a conspiracy to take the throne from his father. Thousands took his side in the attempted overthrow, and it came to a final showdown in the woods near the river Jordan.

There, as Absalom was riding a mule, the animal *"went under the thick boughs of a great oak, and his head caught hold of the oak, and he was taken up between the heaven and the earth; and the mule that was under him went away"* (2 Samuel 18:9).

While he was hanging, Joab *"took three darts in his hand, and thrust them through the heart of*

Absalom" (verse 14). Thousands of Absalom's men were slaughtered and David retained his throne.

This was the tragic fate of a man who gave his word to serve the Lord but broke his vow.

Can a Vow Be Canceled?

I was once asked, "Should a husband and wife make a vow together, or should it be an individual matter?"

When it comes to the giving of money that involves the household finances, it should be a mutual decision whenever possible.

In fact, there is instruction in the Bible which warns against a woman making a monetary vow without the consent of her father (if single) or her husband. Scripture says the man can actually cancel such a vow.

The first time I read this to Suzanne, she was surprised to find it written in the Bible.

——— ≈ ———

The first time I read this to Suzanne, she was surprised to find it written in the Bible.

124

God told Moses to gather the leaders of the tribes of Israel and give them this command: *"When a man makes a vow to the LORD or takes an oath to obligate himself by a pledge, he must not break his word but must do everything he said. When a young woman still living in her father's house makes a vow to the LORD or obligates herself by a pledge and her father hears about her vow or pledge but says nothing to her, then all her vows and every pledge by which she obligated herself will stand. But if her father forbids her when he hears about it, none of her vows or the pledges by which she obligated herself will stand; the LORD will release her because her father has forbidden her"* (Numbers 30:2-5, NIV).

Concerning a married woman, *"If she marries after she makes a vow or after her lips utter a rash promise by which she obligates herself and her husband hears about it but says nothing to her, then her vows or the pledges by which she obligated herself will stand. But if her husband forbids her when he hears about it, he nullifies the vow that obligates her or the rash promise by which she obligates herself, and the LORD will release her"* (verses 6-8, NIV).

These are not my words; they are God's!

The Power of Agreement

Being in unity, however, is far better than discord. To foster harmony in the home, the Lord says, *"Two shall be one"* (Ephesians 5:31).

When a husband and wife together make a vow, heaven will respond to this power of agreement.

Certainly there are times when we make a personal commitment to the Lord because we want our spouse to be at peace concerning some issue. But in the vast majority of family matters, when you join together, the vow becomes even stronger. As Scripture asks, *"Can two walk together, except they be agreed?"* (Amos 3:3).

Suzanne and I openly talk over the challenges we face in ministry, family, finances, and relationships.

———— ∼ ————

Suzanne and I openly talk over the challenges we face in ministry, family, finances, and relationships.

More than once I have told her, "I believe I need to make a vow to God regarding this matter."

Invariably, she will respond, "I totally agree. You ought to."

There have also been times when I encourage her regarding the commitment she is making to the Lord involving an urgent matter.

"I'll Give Him Back"

In talking with my mother about our family history, I came to the conclusion I probably would not have been born had it not been for a vow!

The first child of my parents was a beautiful girl named Rose. Yet in the Hinn ancestral tradition, the firstborn should have been a son and heir.

My mother heard the biting words from some of the women in her family ringing in her ears. They chided her for her failure to produce a boy. "After all," one of them commented, "each of your other sisters-in-law" had sons.

The jeering and mocking often reduced my mother to tears. She felt embarrassment and shame.

At that time my parents were living in two different cities because of the conflict between the

Arabs and the Jews. My mother's family lived in the West Bank town of Ramallah, while my father's relatives resided in Jaffa, near the sea. As a consequence, they could not see each other for the entire year, except for a few days each Christmas.

Finally, my mother was given the necessary paperwork to live in Jaffa with my father—and she soon became pregnant with a second child.

In a labor room of the hospital overlooking the Mediterranean Sea, Clemence Hinn looked out the window and, with her eyes gazing heavenward, said, "Lord, I have only one request. If You will give me a boy, I will give him back to You."

On December 3, 1952, I entered this world. And my mother never recanted her vow. At every step of my spiritual journey, she encouraged and prayed for my future—truly giving me to the Lord.

Willing to Die!

The making of covenants with God goes back thousands of years in church history, because people understood the Lord not only loves to hear our vows, but He also answers them!

This was not something hidden from the people of Israel. It was demonstrated by spiritual leadership and entered into repeatedly by those who needed an answer from the Almighty.

The biblical practice continued in New Testament times. For example, the people warned the apostle Paul that if he preached in Jerusalem, the authorities might have him arrested or even killed. But Paul made a vow to go to the city, saying, *"For I am ready not to be bound only, but also to die at Jerusalem for the name of the Lord Jesus"* (Acts 21:13).

An Act of Worship

What we are discussing is more than an exercise in "proving God." David saw it as an act of worship. He exclaimed, *"Praise waiteth for thee, O God, in Sion: and unto thee shall the vow be performed"* (Psalm 65:1).

A commitment to the Father is not to be entered into by one person here or another family there—it is for the entire church!

Don't Change Your Mind!

Scripture warns, *"When you make a vow to God, do not delay in fulfilling it. He has no pleasure in fools; fulfill your vow. It is better not to vow than to make a vow and not fulfill it"* (Ecclesiastes 5:4-5, NIV).

The headline in these verses is: Don't dare change your mind!

———— ∾ ————

The headline in these verses is: Don't dare change your mind!

What are the consequences of reneging on your promise? God considers it sin. *"Do not let your mouth lead you into sin. And do not protest to the* [angel], *'My vow was a mistake.' Why should God be angry at what you say and destroy the work of your hands?"* (verse 6, NIV).

If you want to avoid pain, suffering, and destruction, faithfully keep the commitments you make to your heavenly Father.

Put Your Faith to the Test

Perhaps, as you are reading these words you realize you have never truly made a significant, meaningful vow to the Lord. Oh, during a momentary crisis you may have made some hasty promises to God, but as you look back, they were insignificant, and you might not even remember what you said.

Do you truly believe your heavenly Father is a vow-answering God? If you do, why not put your faith and His ability to the test?

———— ∽ ————

Do you truly believe your heavenly Father is a vow-answering God? If you do, why not put your faith and His ability to the test?

In the past you may have prayed, interceded, agreed, and fasted for the mountain you face to be removed. Now it is time to make your vow and see God perform a miracle.

But when the Lord answers, don't dare forget the pledge you have made.

Returning God's Favor

At a moment when only the Lord could come to his rescue, David made a promise to God from his heart (Psalm 66:13-14). Then, when the time of trouble was ended, he was faithful to his word, asking, *"What shall I render unto the LORD for all his benefits toward me?"* (Psalm 116:12).

Answering his own question, David declared, *"I will pay my vows unto the LORD now in the presence of all his people"* (verse 14). This was so important, he actually repeated the statement twice (verse 18).

Never forget there are two distinct parts to the agreement—the promise and the performance: *"Vow, and pay unto the LORD your God"* (Psalm 76:11). To say it another way, a vow must be *made* for it to be *paid!*

Again and again we are told, *"Offer unto God thanksgiving; and pay thy vows unto the most High"* (Psalm 50:14).

Don't view this as a duty but a delight. God has been gracious to you and you are returning the favor by being generous with Him.

I pray the Lord is lifting your faith at this very moment to make a significant vow so you will be a recipient of "The Gift" He has planned.

10

THE GIFT IS
ON ITS WAY!

I smile every time I see a Christmas nativity scene with three wise men on camels placed beside the lowly manger in Bethlehem. Yes, there were three kinds of gifts presented to the Christ child, but nowhere in Scripture does it state there were only *three* wise men.

In fact, the events surrounding the birth of our Savior speak of an incredible outpouring of God's abundance during this world-changing event.

When these men of old arrived in Jerusalem, there must have been a great many of them because they shook the city. Not only was Herod troubled, but *"all Jerusalem with him"* (Matthew 2:3).

In those days, the city had a population of

135

approximately two hundred fifty thousand—not a small village. Three visitors dressed in Babylonian attire would hardly be noticed, much less cause an uproar in bustling Jerusalem.

Some Bible scholars have suggested those who came could have numbered in the thousands!

Gifts of Gold

When you study Scripture, you find there may have been years between the time of Jesus's birth and the arrival of the wise men. He was already a young lad, not an infant.

Instead of arriving at the manger, the Bible states, *"When they were come into the house, they saw the young child with Mary his mother, and fell down, and worshipped him"* (Matthew 2:11).

At *"the house,"* who did they see? It was a *"young child."*

The word *child* in the Greek is *pais*, which means a child older than a *brethos*, or "newborn."

Then *"when they had opened their treasures, they presented unto him gifts; gold, and frankincense, and myrrh"* (verse 11).

136

These weren't just three small trinkets, but *treasures* presented to Jesus. The gifts they offered were not meager or hastily thought of; they were significant:

- The frankincense depicted the Lord's royal position.
- The myrrh spoke of His death, suffering, and resurrection.
- The gold represented His divinity.

Scripture makes it clear there was, at the every least, a period of two years between the time the wise men saw the child and failed to report the birth to Herod—as he had requested (Matthew 2:8). That is why Herod demanded the slaughter of *"all the children that were in Bethlehem, and in all the coasts thereof, from two years old and under"* (verse 16).

Enough for the Journey

Some historians believe it may have taken as long as twelve years for the wise men to reach Bethlehem from the time they first saw the guiding star in their eastern nations.

Another reason the wise men brought gold is because God knew Joseph, Mary, and Jesus were about to escape to Egypt and needed sufficient finances to last for the years of the journey.

We can only draw this conclusion: at the start of Christ's life on earth, there was an amazing transfer of wealth.

———— ∽ ————

We can only draw this conclusion: at the start of Christ's life on earth, there was an amazing transfer of wealth.

Unlocking the Floodgates

Today, it is impossible to calculate the incredible blessings God is waiting to pour on those who are prepared to receive them. As Scripture records, *"He that is of a proud heart stirreth up strife: but he that putteth his trust in the LORD shall be made fat"* (Proverbs 28:25).

This "fatness" has nothing to do with our physical weight; rather it is the amazing abundance the Lord has in store for us.

Remember, it is our total trust in the Lord that unlocks the floodgates.

Even though the wealth of the world will be placed in the hands of the righteous, those who qualify as recipients must be free from the "love" of money. As Scripture declares, *"He that loveth silver shall not be satisfied with silver; nor he that loveth abundance with increase: this is also vanity"* (Ecclesiastes 5:10).

Abundance is an automatic byproduct of our obedience to the Lord—not the result of seeking riches: *"If they obey and serve him, they shall spend their days in prosperity, and their years in pleasures"* (Job 36:11).

A Heaven-Directed Plan

God's transfer of riches is spoken of repeatedly. For example, we are told, *"For God giveth to a man that is good in his sight wisdom, and knowledge, and joy: but to the sinner he giveth travail, to gather and to heap*

up, that he may give to him that is good before God"
(Ecclesiastes 2:26).

Why is the sinner allowed to "gather and to heap
up"? It is so the Lord can transfer this wealth "to him
that is good before God"—the obedient, the trusting,
the faithful.

We should not take the statement lightly in which
the Lord proclaims He "giveth thee power to get
wealth" (Deuteronomy 8:18). This means there is a
supernatural, God-given, heaven-directed plan for you
to prosper.

Even more, when the Almighty produces your
abundance, your very soul will be satisfied.

Take It Back!

The earth belongs to the Lord (Psalm 24:2)—and
everything Satan owns has been given to him by man.
The devil produces nothing by himself. This means,
since man has given Satan what he possesses, we can
take it back "by force" (Matthew 11:12).

The enemy has been stealing from the saints, and
it's time for this wealth to be returned. In the words of

Jesus, *"The thief cometh not, but for to steal, and to kill, and to destroy: I am come that they might have life, and that they might have it more abundantly"* (John 10:10).

A God of Plenty

Scripture speaks of a storehouse (Malachi 3:10) where you place your overflow after all your needs are met. The Lord doesn't skimp and just barely meet your basic requirements. He is a God of plenty, providing far beyond what you can ask or think.

———— ∾ ————

The Lord doesn't skimp and just barely meet your basic requirements. He is a God of plenty, providing far beyond what you can ask or think.

Remember, the righteous man leaves *"an inheritance to his children's children"* (Proverbs 13:22). Even your great-grandchildren will enjoy what you have been blessed with by God.

Miracles in the Desert

Earlier I discussed how the children of Israel walked out of Egypt as millionaires. The biggest miracle, however, is the fact they didn't have to spend their riches on food or clothing. Not only did God provide manna from heaven for them to eat, but miraculously their shoes or garments did not wear out for forty years (Deuteronomy 29:5)!

Even more amazing, some of them left the land of Pharaoh as little children. That means their shoes and clothes actually *grew* while they were wearing them. Wow!

They didn't even have to pay for a light bill because their was a fire to lead the way by night.

I'm sure some of them said, "Why do we need all this money?"

To that God must have replied, "Just enjoy My abundance!"

It Belongs to Us!

There may be problems in distribution, but there is certainly no shortage of food or other resources in the world God created. Not only is the whole earth full of His glory (Isaiah 6:3), it is *"full of thy riches"* (Psalm 104:24).

Many years ago I heard it said that not one dime has ever left the planet since Adam. It is simply recycled, and the billions are still here. Thank God, we are about to receive this bounty! It's the Lord's, and it belongs to His people.

———— ≈ ————

Thank God, we are about to receive this bounty!
It's the Lord's, and it belongs to His people.

Takers vs. Givers

It took me a long time to fully learn that the man who devours his seed remains poor, while the one who plants is rewarded beyond measure.

Let's face the facts. The devil's system is one based on *taking*—which, sadly, he has successfully embedded in our carnal nature. He is always stealing and hoarding for his own selfish desires, and he's prodding us to do the same.

Demons love to gain control of your body, your mind, your money, and your health—and they fight to retain and hold on to what they have captured.

———— ∽ ————

Demons love to gain control of your body, your mind, your money, and your health—and they fight to retain and hold on to what they have captured.

When we came into this world we were born in sin and *"shapen in iniquity"* (Psalm 51:5). Only through the new birth experience with Christ are we freed from Satan's grip.

Any man or woman who is not a true giver is telling God Almighty and the whole world, "I am still bound by the old nature of selfishness."

What a contrast Satan is from our "giving" Father who takes such pleasure in showering His children with the riches of heaven. Remember, God so loved that world *"that he gave"* His only begotten Son (John 3:16).

For Your Good

When you sow scripturally, God touches your hand supernaturally and it becomes like a magnet, pulling back what is in the devil's hand.

Suddenly, you receive favor from people you don't even know. As Joseph experienced when he went from the pit to the palace, what you thought was meant for evil turns out for your good.

Your future may appear dismal and bleak, but rest in His promises. God is about to turn things around!

Seven Gifts of Blessing

The Word assures us that when we give according to His command, He proves His promises by returning far more to us than we ever expect.

Here is the glorious exchange He offers: *"Bring ye all the tithes into the storehouse, that there may be meat in mine house, and prove me now herewith, saith the LORD of hosts, if I will not open you the windows of heaven, and pour you out a blessing, that there shall not be room enough to receive it. And I will rebuke the devourer for your sakes, and he shall not destroy the fruits of your ground; neither shall your vine cast her fruit before the time in the field, saith the LORD of hosts. And all nations shall call you blessed: for ye shall be a delightsome land"* (Malachi 3:10-12).

In this marvelous portion of Scripture, there are seven gifts of blessing God is ready to bestow on the faithful giver:

Gift #1: The windows of heaven will open.

Revival is imminent, and God will not hold anything back! *"The LORD shall open unto thee his good treasure, the heaven to give the rain unto thy land in his season, and to bless all the work of thine hand"* (Deuteronomy 28:12).

Gift #2: God will pour out a blessing.

This means you will literally be drenched with prosperity, abundance, and the Father's favor: *"For I will pour water upon him that is thirsty, and floods upon the dry ground: I will pour my spirit upon thy seed, and my blessing upon thine offspring"* (Isaiah 44:3).

Gift #3: You will have God's divine protection.

The Lord promises that when you give, *He "will rebuke the devourer"* (Malachi 3:11).

The word *devourer* connects to the physical rather than the emotional part of your being. Your very life, including what you possess, will be guarded by God Himself. Remember, Satan *"as a roaring lion, walketh about, seeking whom he may devour"* (1 Peter 5:8).

Your giving shields you from the adversary—the seed-eater.

Gift #4: God will not allow the enemy to destroy your finances.

When you obey the Lord in the matter of money, the enemy *"shall not destroy the fruits of your ground"* (Malachi 3:11).

In Old Testament times, the economy was based primarily on agriculture, and a horde of hungry locusts could quickly ravage a field of grain, or plunderers could rob a vineyard. In return for obeying His Word, the Lord promised for this "fruit" to remain secure and valuable.

Gift #5: Your family will be protected.

Your heavenly Father also makes this pledge: *"Neither shall your vine cast her fruit before the time in the field"* (Malachi 3:11).

This pertains to your family and your children. Jesus said, *"I am the vine, ye are the branches. He that abideth in me, and I in him, the same bringeth forth much fruit: for without me ye can do nothing"* (John 15:5).

The Lord is carefully watching over what you have planted.

Gift #6: All nations will call you blessed.

The world will be envious as you become a testimony of the Lord's favor. Thankfully, this gives you the opportunity to proclaim what God has done in your life.

Gift #7: The Lord will mightily use you.

As a direct result of your giving, God says, *"Ye shall be a delightsome land"* (Malachi 3:12). The word *delightsome* means "highly desired" in the Hebrew.

Because of your obedience, God will abundantly use you in His kingdom.

They Will Listen

At this very moment there are people in this nation who have never read the Bible or heard the story of redemption through God's Son. These include powerful individuals who know next to nothing concerning the Christian life. It is completely foreign to them.

When I speak to people of influence concerning God and the Gospel, they pay attention only out of politeness, but that's about all. The day is coming, however, when they will listen for one major reason: we will have what is closest to their heart—their wealth!

We Have a Choice

As the Bible teaches, *"Wisdom is better than strength: nevertheless the poor man's wisdom is despised, and his words are not heard"* (Ecclesiastes 9:16).

Nobody wants to hear people who can't back up what they are saying. In the day of this divine wealth exchange, however, the riches of the sinners will be in our hands. And you can be assured others will take notice. The Lord is going to trust you with the preaching of the Gospel—and so much more.

───── ∿ ─────

The Lord is going to trust you with the preaching of the Gospel—and so much more.

So, every day we have a choice to make. Are we going to eat our seed or sow our seed? Are we going to prove to God we are trustworthy followers or not?

The Almighty has created spiritual laws which determine who receives wealth and who remains in poverty. When you obey these covenants, you obtain the benefits and blessings of heaven. But rejecting these divine laws keeps you both spiritually and financially stagnant, struggling through life.

Follow His Directions

Solomon observed what happened to a man who chose the wrong path: *"I went by the field of the* slothful, and by the vineyard of the man void of understanding; And, lo, it was all grown over with thorns, and nettles had covered the face thereof, and the stone wall thereof was broken down. Then I saw, and considered it well: I looked upon it, and received instruction. Yet a little sleep, a little slumber, a little folding of the hands to sleep" (Proverbs 24:30-33).

What is the result of such apathy? "So shall thy poverty come as one that travelleth; and thy want as an armed man" (verse 34).

A life of lack and want descends on those who say, "I refuse to follow God's Word."

Scripture clearly states, "Poverty and shame shall be to him that refuseth instruction: but he that regardeth reproof shall be honoured" (Proverbs 13:18).

The "reproof" spoken of is discipline and correction. These are easy adjustments when you are sensitive to the voice of the Spirit, but difficult indeed for the person who is self-willed and ego driven.

According to the Word, "Correction is grievous unto him that forsaketh the way: and he that hateth reproof shall die" (Proverbs 15:10).

It Is Yours

You may ask, "How close are we to this glorious time of God's wealth transfer?"

The Bible tells us it is part of the last days, and the moment is at hand. James wrote, *"Go to now, ye rich men, weep and howl for your miseries that shall come upon you. Your riches are corrupted, and your garments are motheaten. Your gold and silver is cankered; and the rust of them shall be a witness against you, and shall eat your flesh as it were fire. Ye have heaped treasure together for the last days"* (James 5:1-3).

God is preparing to open those treasures and say, "My people, it is yours!" And we will use these unlimited resources to preach and spread the Gospel of the kingdom to the nations of the world.

"Eye hath not seen, nor ear heard, neither have entered into the heart of man, the things which God hath prepared for them that love him" (1 Corinthians 2:9).

The Gift is on its way!